Y0-AUM-664

"So do not fear, for I am with you;
do not be dismayed, for I am your God.
I will strengthen you and help you;
I will uphold you with my righteous right hand."

—Isaiah 41:10 (niv)

SECRETS From GRANDMA'S ATTIC

History Lost and Found
The Art of Deception

SECRETS From GRANDMA'S ATTIC

THE ART of DECEPTION

Becky Melby

Guideposts

Secrets from Grandma's Attic is a trademark of Guideposts.

Published by Guideposts Books & Inspirational Media
100 Reserve Road, Suite E200
Danbury, CT 06810
Guideposts.org

Copyright © 2022 by Guideposts. All rights reserved.

This book, or parts thereof, may not be reproduced, stored in a retrieval system, or transmitted in any form or by any means, electronic, mechanical, photocopying, recording, or otherwise, without the written permission of the publisher.

This is a work of fiction. While the setting of Secrets from Grandma's Attic as presented in this series is fictional, the location of Canton, Missouri, actually exists, and some places and characters may be based on actual places and people whose identities have been used with permission or fictionalized to protect their privacy. Apart from the actual people, events, and locales that figure into the fiction narrative, all other names, characters, businesses, and events are the creation of the author's imagination and any resemblance to actual persons or events is coincidental.

Every attempt has been made to credit the sources of copyrighted material used in this book. If any such acknowledgment has been inadvertently omitted or miscredited, receipt of such information would be appreciated.

Scripture references are from the following sources: *The Holy Bible, King James Version* (KJV). *The Holy Bible, New International Version* (NIV). Copyright ©1973, 1978, 1984, 2011 by Biblica, Inc. Used by permission of Zondervan. All rights reserved worldwide. www.zondervan.com.

Cover and interior design by Müllerhaus
Cover illustration by Greg Copeland at Illustration Online LLC.
Typeset by Aptara, Inc.

Printed and bound in the United States of America
10 9 8 7 6 5 4 3 2 1

THE ART of DECEPTION

Chapter One

"Whoever said Disney is the happiest place on earth has never been to a flea market!"

Amy Allen laughed at her cousin's unbridled enthusiasm as she stepped out of her sister's air-conditioned car and gasped in the smothering heat. St. Louis was always hot in July, but not this hot.

She passed an antique mirror leaning against a table piled high with old dishes and lace doilies and caught a glimpse of her humidity-frizzed mane. She paused long enough to sweep her thick, damp hair off her neck and twist it into a messy bun.

Amy's sister, Tracy, slid out of the driver's side, not a wrinkle in her crisp sleeveless blouse, not a frizz in her sleek brown hair.

Their cousin Robin lunged out of the back seat, grinning as she slipped her arms into the straps of a mesh backpack. "Come on, ladies. Our Saturday is slipping away. Treasures await."

As Amy scanned row after row of vendor tables and the food trucks that surrounded them like a circle of covered wagons, she wiped the beads of perspiration dotting her top lip. They'd started forming before she'd gotten out of the car. Hot flash. Another reminder of nature's ticking clock. She checked her phone for the hundredth time since leaving home, then said a quick prayer, once again asking God for the call that could change her life and her foster children's future.

"It'll happen," Tracy whispered next to her ear.

Amy slid her phone into her back pocket and gave her sister her biggest, brightest, anxiety-hiding smile. "I know."

"Today is all about distraction, so let's get on with it."

"Right. Onward." Amy pointed to the aisle of tables on their left. "Start there and move right?" She directed the question to Robin, who owned an antique store in Canton. Though bargain hunting was high on Robin's "favorite things" list, it was still work. "Or should we just do random today?"

"I vote for random," Robin said, practically vibrating with anticipation like a runner on the starting block. "And whimsy and serendipity and all things unplanned."

"Sounds like a plan." Amy winked and all three of them laughed. This together time carved out of schedules crammed with kids and work was something they'd all given a higher priority to since Grandma Pearl's passing in December. In Grandma's words, "Family time is a gift worth fighting for."

Amy lagged behind the other two, stopping at a table filled with hand-carved wooden figurines and old maps. Several maps were framed, but most were simply rolled up. Some of the yellowed rolls seemed almost too brittle to touch. Amy grimaced. This was not the way to treat old documents that should be protected from direct sunlight and this intense heat.

She smiled at the man perched on a stool behind the table, whittling a piece of wood. Horn-rimmed glasses, unkempt hair, a white cotton dress shirt that had apparently never been introduced to an iron. She caught a whiff of smoke and could imagine him holding a pipe he'd carved himself.

What was the man's story? Retired college professor? Or maybe he was a real-life Indiana Jones, minus the rugged good looks. Her imagination began to spin a story she could use in her new classroom come fall. *Once there was a curious little man who wore big, round glasses and—*

"Amy! Look at this!" Robin held up a green dish. Depression glass.

Amy strode down the aisle. A closer look at the piece made her heart squeeze. It was exactly like the one they'd found, cracked in two, in Grandma's attic. As Robin held it in her right hand, the sun gave a satin sheen to a pearl ring in a silver filigree setting, an inheritance from their grandmother. The sight brought a tightening in Amy's chest. More than six months had passed since December 26—the day Grandma Pearl died less than twenty-four hours after her one-hundredth birthday—yet the loss still seemed fresh at times. Amy stemmed the wave of emotion with a deep breath.

Robin moved on to look at an old wooden ice cream maker, but Amy felt drawn back to the maps. The man smiled. "A fellow cartophile, I see."

"Yes. I'm a teacher." She slowly unrolled one of the scrolls. An intricate border of twined ivy framed a city map, blocks laid out in neat squares dissected by streets. She read the name on a horizontal street. *Penrose.* Her heart rate climbed. Just below it, a large square, labeled in block letters. *Hyde Park.*

Goose bumps skittered up both arms. An old St. Louis map. She didn't want to risk opening it farther, but it had to be from the 1800s.

She set it down gently and picked up another. A map of the Mississippi River drawn in 1867. Another of Jefferson City from 1892. Did this man have any idea what he possessed here? She was about to ask what he'd charge for the whole lot when a simple, hand-drawn map drew her attention. This one wasn't rolled up—it was lying flat on the table. Two faintly scrawled words caught her eye right away. *Clark Street.*

Not an uncommon street name. And yet... She moved in for a closer inspection. Not paper, but canvas. Why would someone draw a sloppy map on thick, quality cloth instead of paper? After asking permission, she picked it up, turned so the sun was at her back, and held it high enough to keep her shadow from blocking the light as she examined the penciled grid. Familiar streets. And at the top, the name of the town she'd just moved back to. *Canton, Missouri.*

"How in the world—" Tracy's gasp yanked Amy's gaze away from the pencil lines. Tracy and Robin stood in front of her, staring at the other side of the map.

"That's an exact replica!" Robin said, pointing at the canvas Amy held.

Confused, Amy turned the map so she could see the other side, almost dropping it in the process.

A painting covered what she now realized was the front of the canvas. A very familiar painting. That profile. That dress. She was staring at an oil painting she'd seen many, many times. Only once this close.

"This is not a replica, ladies, I assure you," Indiana Jones said.

Tracy shook her head, as if trying to clear it. "Green Girl," she whispered.

It was the name the three of them had given to the beautiful girl in the green velvet dress trimmed with white lace in the painting that had hung above Grandma Pearl's fireplace mantel for decades. The girl was a mystery that sparked questions Grandma always answered with a cryptic smile and, "Who do you think she is?"

Oh, the stories they'd concocted to answer that question. Grandma Pearl told them Green Girl was indeed a real person, someone she had known well, but that was all she would divulge.

"If this isn't a copy," Robin whispered, "then Grandma's is. We have to buy it. We have to compare it to—"

Amy's sharp inhale stopped Robin's words. She pointed to the bottom right corner as the other two came to stand beside her. A small red *A* marred Green Girl's pinky finger. "I did that," Amy said, excitement building in her voice. "I was five or six, I think. I heard Tracy ask Grandma why the artist's name wasn't on the painting. I started putting my own name on it so I could pretend I was the artist. It's the only time I ever remember Grandma raising her voice. She was so upset. I think she started crying. I know I did."

"How did it get here?" Robin asked.

Amy very carefully laid the painting back on the table. "She wouldn't have parted with it." Grandma's overstuffed attic was proof she hadn't easily let go of anything. "She would never have sold it."

"She might have gifted it," Robin suggested.

Amy felt her eyes smart. "But why not to one of us? Or someone else in the family? When's the last time you remember it hanging above the fireplace?"

"It's been years. I'd guess thirty, at least," Tracy said.

Amy lowered her voice. "We have to buy it. What's it worth, Robin?"

In a conspiratorial whisper, Robin answered, "To us, priceless. To him…who knows? We kind of blew it by letting him know how much it means to us. I want to ask him where he got it, but not until we make a deal. Maybe we need to appeal to his sympathies. Amy, you're the best at that. Turn on the charm, girl."

Amy didn't have to fake the emotion, but she decided to start with a professional approach. "How much are you asking for this?"

Indiana Jones rubbed his stubbled chin. "For you, eight hundred dollars."

Amy swallowed hard and tried to hide her shock. "It's not signed. Or framed," she added weakly.

"But it's clearly very old and in excellent condition."

No thanks to your storage methods. The smell of smoke permeated the canvas. Up close, it didn't really smell like tobacco smoke, but she couldn't be sure. "As you can probably tell, this painting means a great deal to our family. It belonged to our dear, departed grandmother." Tracy's elbow jab signaled she'd laid it on a bit too thick, but she could tell she had the man's attention. "Clearly you have an appreciation for things with a history. Do you have anything that belonged to your grandparents?"

The man's smile seemed to sag. "Nah. My mama was a very practical woman. I remember asking her if I could have the wooden box my granddaddy kept his glasses in. She said it was old and useless and I was being ridiculous, and she threw it away." His voice grew rough. "How about I give it to you for three hundred?"

Amy wanted to protest that it should rightly belong to them anyway, but Robin cut in before she had time to voice her frustration.

"Deal." Robin dug in her purse and pulled out three crisp hundred-dollar bills. "Now, can you tell us where you got it?"

"Sure. See that empty table over there?" He pointed across the aisle. "A young woman, early twenties, I'd guess, has been here every weekend since we opened for the season. She was an artist, a painter, and a potter. Did good work, selling her paintings and pottery. She was the shy type, but I got her gabbing enough to find out she's an art student trying to earn tuition money. I bought a few pieces from her, just to help out. Then last Saturday—wasn't even noon yet—she starts packing up real quick like, then runs over with this canvas and says she's got a family emergency and has to sell it fast. Pretty crude map, but when I saw the painting on the other side and how scared she was, I just had to do what I could for the poor thing, you know?"

And get a good deal by taking advantage of her situation. Amy felt her jaw tighten. They'd probably just been swindled big time. But at least they had the painting.

"Why do you think she was scared?" Robin asked.

"Can't say. But there was something strange goin' on, I tell you. Something really strange."

Amy's knees hurt from kneeling on the wide-planked floor of Grandma Pearl's attic on Wednesday morning. Tracy and her husband, Jeff, owned the house now. But until they got around to sorting through decades' worth of boxes, Amy could only think of this room as Grandma's attic.

Four days had passed since the flea market. Between school physicals and clothes shopping, she hadn't had time to think about the painting. Now, in the quiet of the attic, she looked around, wondering where they should start searching for clues that might tell them how it ended up at a flea market in St. Louis.

She stretched her back then pulled a cobweb out of her hair. Her neck ached from leaning over a box of old photos, sorting them into piles by year. She should have listened to Tracy and taken them down to the dining room, but this dusty, musty-smelling space brought back such wonderful memories of dressing up in their mother's old bridesmaid gowns, playing hide-and-seek with Tracy and Robin, and standing before an antique oval mirror holding Grandma's wedding dress in front of her and dreaming of the day she'd walk down the aisle wearing her satin and lace "something old."

That dream was growing as faded as some of the photographs spread out before her. Whoever came up with the word "bittersweet" certainly understood the range of emotions she felt at the moment.

The call hadn't come yet. Melanie, their caseworker, assured her they'd hear something soon.

Ten-year-old Matt and six-year-old Jana, her foster children she hoped to adopt, had the same mother, but different fathers. Their mother, Janelle, a woman Amy had met twice, dropped out of drug rehab for the third time three months ago. Matt's father was in prison and had no interest in being a dad, but just when Janelle said she was ready to relinquish her parental rights, Jana's father had unexpectedly shown up, after disappearing from Jana's life when she was four. Now Janelle was holding off on signing over her rights, hoping for a future with her ex. A future Melanie wasn't encouraging.

Amy glanced at her watch. Half an hour until she had to pick up the kids from Vacation Bible School. More mixed emotions. While she missed them whenever she wasn't with them, she hadn't realized, before becoming a foster mom, the value of time alone to think and pray and regroup. And this was the perfect place for all of that.

Sitting back on her heels, she rubbed the small of her back and looked around. Dust motes did pirouettes in the shaft of feeble sunlight straining through the smeared west window. Wood crates and cardboard boxes filled with knickknacks and every receipt or warranty that had ever passed through their grandfather's hands towered between random pieces of shrouded, outdated, or in-need-of-repair furniture. So much family history yet to be uncovered.

"You about done?" Tracy's voice preceded her up the stairs. She must be home on lunch break from her job at the newspaper.

"Almost. One more box and then I have to go get the kids." She reached inside the bin she'd been emptying and brought out a flat, hinged black box. She held it up to Tracy. "What's your guess? I'm going with something from Tiffany's. A gift to Grandma from her first love, a soldier who died in the war. Velvet-lined with a necklace of solid diamonds we can sell to finish all of our remodeling dreams."

Tracy rolled her eyes. "I'm going with clippings from our first haircuts. Or maybe our baby teeth."

"That's disgusting!"

"But realistic." Tracy motioned for her to open it.

Amy eased the top open then let out a sigh of feigned disappointment. The box was, indeed, lined in velvet, but contained a couple of envelopes and folded pieces of paper. Dark fingerprints smudged the outside of the first one. Amy opened it. "It's a receipt." She held it out so Tracy could read over her shoulder.

Wolfram & Randulph Fine Arts
1202 South 7th Street, St. Louis, Missouri
December 25, 1937
RE: A Study in Emerald Velvet - $45 payment

Tracy's sharp inhale echoed Amy's. "Study in Emerald Velvet. Could that be Green Girl?" Excitement laced her words as she peered over Amy's shoulder. "Grandma paid forty-five dollars for it on Christmas Day in 1937. Maybe it was a birthday present to herself."

Amy studied the paper. "No. Look." She pointed to the next line. "Part of this is smudged, but it says, 'Record of Payment to P. Wallace for…' something. I can't make it out, but it's probably the name of the painting, right? So Grandma didn't pay the gallery. The gallery paid Grandma."

Tracy took the paper from her and squinted at it. "She sold it to them? But that doesn't make sense. If she sold it, why was it hanging in her house all those years? What else is in the box?"

Amy picked up one of the envelopes and turned it over. The only thing written on it was *Pearl* in a wispy blue script. She opened the flap and pulled out an age-brittled clipping from the *Canton Times*.

Painting Stolen
Sometime between the hours of 10 p.m. Wednesday and
6 a.m. Thursday, thieves broke into a Canton home and stole

a 3-foot by 4-foot painting. Police report signs of forced entry. Homeowner was home at the time. Details are being withheld pending further investigation.

"Is there a date?"

Amy turned the paper over. "Nothing but an ad for the Sizzlin' Griddle."

"That's been around since before Mom was born. That's no help." Tracy tucked her hair behind her ears. "Is it a leap to assume the painting that was stolen was Green Girl?"

"Maybe. But why else would Grandma have kept these papers together? We have to do some digging. Where do we start?"

Suddenly seeing this mystery as another welcome gift of distraction, Amy grinned at her. "We start where we always start." And then, in unison they said, "We call Robin."

Chapter Two

"She's back where she belongs," Amy said two days later, as she, Tracy, and Robin stood in front of the white-painted fireplace inlaid with green subway tiles, staring up at the painting on the mantel. Robin's friend Claire, a freelance artist and graphic designer, had carefully tacked it to stretcher bars and cleaned it. The smoke smell was almost gone. Robin had used her lunch break to bring it over. They'd all agreed Green Girl's place was right here in the family room where she'd been throughout their childhood. "And she looks pretty good for her age."

Tracy nodded. "But a little underdressed without a frame."

"I'll keep looking," Robin said. "I have a plain black one at the store that would fit, but it just wouldn't do her justice. She does look good."

The girl in the green velvet dress sat on a bench with elaborately carved legs, facing a painting that hung on the wall. Her face was seen in silhouette, lending a mystique to her that had always intrigued the girls. They guessed she was in her teens or early twenties, but it was hard to tell from the angle the painter had chosen. The hand that rested on the bench sported a large emerald ring in a gold filigree setting. Her mahogany-colored hair was chin length and curled at the bottom, held back from her face by a band of small daisies. The daisies coordinated with the painting she appeared to be studying, of a young girl in a long white nightgown holding a bouquet of daisies.

"Do you think she's Grandma Pearl?" Robin's voice sounded wistful.

Tracy shook her head. "Don't you remember when we asked her?"

Amy couldn't forget that moment. "She laughed and said we'd been reading way too many fairy tales."

"She said she could only dream of being that beautiful," Tracy added.

"And rich enough to have a ring like that," Amy continued. "That's when we decided Green Girl must be a princess, and I wrote that dreadful play, *The Sad Princess in the Locked Tower*." Amy put her hand over her heart and sighed. "I have no idea why my playwriting career ended so soon."

"I loved my part," Robin said dryly. "I got to be the girl with the daisies." She nudged Amy with her shoulder. "Green Girl's twin sister who dies tragically when she falls off the castle balcony and drowns in the mote."

Amy laughed. "Maybe it was a tad melodramatic."

"Ya think?" Tracy's smile showed off the dimple in her right cheek. "But I loved playing the princess who locks herself in the tower when her sister dies and won't come out until the handsome prince climbs the trellis and rescues her." She wrinkled her nose. "Grandma's friend Miss Blair was visiting when we did the play."

"I have a vague recollection of being scared of her," Robin said.

"She never smiled. Grandma gushed at our performance, but Miss Blair just sat there, stone-faced. I do remember her saying our story was nothing like the real one. When I asked her to tell us more, she just shook her head and went upstairs." Tracy waved her hand in front of her as if to brush away the memory. "Anyway, the Green Girl is still a princess in my mind. And I can't think of her as *A Study in Emerald Velvet*."

"Nope." Robin shook her head. "She'll always be Green Girl to us."

Amy stepped closer, admiring the intricate swirls and distinct feathery brushstrokes. And the red letter *A* on Green Girl's little finger. "I thought Claire would have removed or covered up my 'signature.'"

Robin shook her head. "I told her not to. It's part of Green Girl's history."

"Now we just need to figure out the rest of her story." Tracy looked at Robin, then Amy. "Where do we start?"

Robin brushed shiny dark bangs off her forehead. "Claire suggested we research artists who did paintings within paintings. She said it's a trademark for some painters. I did a little looking. It was popular in the Netherlands in the 1600s, but Green Girl can't be that old. Whistler painted his mother with a framed painting in the background in 1871." Robin shrugged. "Just a bit of antique-geek trivia. Anyway, I'm going to do some more searching. It might be a rabbit trail, but I need something to do while I'm waiting at Kai's tae kwon do class."

Amy tapped her chin. "Maybe she's looking at a picture of herself when she was younger. She has such a pondering look on what we can see of her face. Maybe she's reflecting on her childhood."

"Could be," Tracy said. "So, what's next?" As the oldest, Tracy had always taken it upon herself to keep the other two on task.

Those stick-to-the-deadline skills also came in handy in her job as writer of Cantonbury Tales, a column in the Canton newspaper.

"We need to talk to Indiana Jones again," Amy said. "Who's up for a road trip tomorrow?"

Robin's mouth twisted to one side. "Wish I could, but Terry and I promised to take Kai and a few of his friends swimming."

Tracy's expression matched Robin's. "Chad's coming over to help Jeff tile the upstairs bathroom, so Anna and I are taking Corbin and Emerson to the toy museum. You and the kids should come with us."

Amy tried to keep her expression light. "We took some of Matt's friends there last month." Robert Wyatt's collection of over twenty thousand toys was one of her foster son's favorite places, and he and his friends were fascinated with Wyatt's vintage cars from the 1950s and '60s.

The stab of sadness she'd spent years trying to surrender to God opened a fresh wound. Amy was genuinely happy for her sister and cousin, yet sometimes when they prattled on about their busy lives with their beautiful families, she got sucked into a familiar pit where all she could dwell on was what she didn't have.

On Valentine's Day, Tracy and Jeff, a history professor at Canton's Culver-Stockton College, had celebrated their thirtieth wedding anniversary. They had two grown children. Chad and his wife, Anna, were the busy parents of four-year-old Corbin and his little sister, two-year-old Emerson. Tracy and Jeff's daughter, Sara, and her husband, Kevin Willey, had two children. Aiden was two and Zoe, a year old. Robin, younger than Amy by two years, had just celebrated twenty years of marriage to Terry last month. Their son Kai was thirteen.

Amy had been there to rejoice with Tracy and Robin at every birth, birthday, and wedding, yet, with each passing year, it became a little harder to share their joy. She knew it was a selfish attitude, but here she was at forty-eight with no marriage prospects in sight, hoping and praying to become a permanent mom to Matt and Jana, knowing all her dreams could be shattered with a single phone call.

"I'll have a little free time after I close the store this afternoon," Robin said. "I think I'll start asking around town. If we can figure out when the painting was stolen, maybe we can find someone who knows something about it."

"Good idea," Tracy said. "I'll start at the paper. If I can't uncover anything there, I'll move on to the library."

"Maybe I'll take the kids to the flea market and the zoo tomorrow. They'd love that." Amy congratulated herself on keeping her voice steady. "Let me know what questions you have for Indiana Jones."

Tracy put her arm around Amy's shoulders, a move that said she could see through her sister's smile to the pain behind it. "We trust you to get the scoop with your mad teacher skills."

Amy managed to get the kids to bed early on Friday night, then up for breakfast at six and on the road by six thirty—a minor miracle, which got them to the St. Louis Zoo by nine when the temperature was still a relatively cool seventy-eight degrees, on its way to eighty-eight. She promised them three hours at the zoo followed by lunch at Hi Pointe Drive-In.

In order to keep the peace, she divided the morning into fifteen-minute segments of "Jana's Choice" and "Matt's Choice." Every time they switched turns, she wanted to leave a suggestion for the zoo planners, asking them to please put all large animals in one place. The giraffes, located in the zoo's Red Rock section, were Jana's favorite, while Matt could spend his entire time gazing at elephants in the River's Edge section on the opposite side of the park. That meant they couldn't spend a lot of time stopping to look at the monkeys, whose antics always drew their attention. She'd learned that promising them ice cream when they got to River's Edge kept them moving.

By noon they were all hot and tired and ready for an air-conditioned car and lunch. Jana ordered her usual mac and cheese, and Matt, who had announced shortly after his tenth birthday that he was way too old for a kids' menu, asked for the cowboy burger. Eleven dollars, compared to the six-dollar offerings on the kids' menu. *A little foreshadowing of things to come*, Amy thought.

Too hot to think about a burger or fries, she ordered a grilled salmon salad with dried cherries and orange vinaigrette. She hoped that getting to the flea market two hours before closing would mean the crowds had thinned but Indiana wouldn't be packing up yet.

Cooled off and refueled, the kids were excited about a flea market treasure hunt. To Amy's surprise, Matt was intrigued about the mystery of Green Girl and wanted to help solve it.

When they got out of the car, he said, "I have a plan, Mom." He held up the camera Tracy and Jeff had given him for Christmas.

Mom. It still made her gasp sometimes. Matt and Jana had been with her since November. She'd told them they could call her whatever they felt comfortable with, and they had shyly called her "Miss Amy" until Valentine's Day, when Jana handed her a card the two had made together that said, "Thank you for taking care of us, Mom." That card was now framed on her dresser.

Please, God... Those two words were a prayer she breathed often since the day she told the social worker she wanted to start adoption proceedings. She smiled at Matt. "What's your plan, Spymaster?"

"When you talk to Indiana Jones, I'm going to hide behind something and video him. I read about how to tell if people are lying. If he starts scratching or fidgeting, or he looks away when you ask him a question, he's probably lying. Or if he makes hand gestures *after* he says something instead of while he's saying it, that means his brain is so busy making stuff up that it can't make his hands move at the same time. I'll get it all on video and then we can analyze it." He grinned at her.

She couldn't squelch the enthusiasm of this boy who barely smiled for the first six weeks he'd lived with her. "Okay. Just try not to be too obvious." They couldn't arrest a ten-year-old for taking videos of someone without permission. Could they?

Jana held Amy's hand as they walked along the aisles lined with tents and tables crammed with crafts and antiques and someone's junk waiting to be someone else's treasure. When they reached a booth that sold reversible sequin purses and pillows, Jana stopped. It saddened Amy that she didn't yet feel comfortable enough to ask for something like most six-year-olds would. Whether out of fear of being scolded, or resignation that she wouldn't get what she wanted anyway, Amy wasn't sure. While she didn't want to become an overindulgent parent, she also needed to let them know they deserved a bit of spoiling. She led Jana into the U-shaped booth formed by three tables laden with sparkle. "What would you like?"

Wide, questioning eyes met hers, then slowly scanned the brilliance just below Jana's eye level. Finally, after another questioning look, she pointed to a small purple purse with a strap. Amy bought it, then put a dollar in it before handing it to Jana. Through the whole exchange, Amy managed not to get as overly emotional as she often did…until she looked at Matt, who was grinning from ear to ear.

With an arm around each of them, she set off to find Indiana Jones.

"Hey there!" Indiana retreated a step when he saw her. Just surprise? Or guilt? "Welcome back. You come for the maps?"

Amy had almost forgotten about the beautiful old maps. She picked up a rolled parchment, once again cringing at the way they were spread out on the table in the blazing sun where anyone could pick them up. Or knock them on the ground. Though she was pinching pennies, purchasing these maps would be saving a little piece of history. And perusing them would buy her time with him. "Have you sold any?"

"A couple. And it's an interesting coinkydink that a guy came just about an hour ago askin' for that painting you bought." Furrows formed between his shaggy brows.

"He did?" Her pulse quickened. "What did he say when you told him you'd sold it?"

"Wasn't too happy. Mumbled something under his breath and stalked off."

A chill skittered up her spine. "Did you tell him who you sold it to?"

"Hmm." Indiana adjusted his glasses. "Guess I did say I sold it to three women who said it used to belong to their grandma." He pressed his lips together. "Probably shouldn't have said that. Just didn't think."

Had they told Indiana they lived in Canton? She didn't think so. "Did you tell him anything else about us?"

"Nope. That was it."

She breathed a sigh of relief. Yet it still left questions hanging and raised the hairs on the back of her neck. "Is there anything else you can tell me about the woman who gave you the painting?"

"Well, let me think." He tapped his chin with his fingertip. "She's an art student at Culver-Stockton up in Canton."

Amy's throat tightened. She'd assumed the young woman was going to school in St. Louis.

The man reached behind him. "Bought this mug she made. She said she took it out of the kiln the day before." He dumped a trickle of coffee onto the gravel and handed the cup to Amy.

Glazed in cobalt blue and a rich brown, the mug was beautiful. Sunlight caught flecks of copper on the surface. Amy turned it over. Two letters, *NC*, staggered, with the N slightly higher than the C. Next to the letters was the outline of a dragonfly.

A maker's mark. Their first clue.

September 13, 1937

Hiding in my special place again. Mother found out I brought a candle in here and got really angry, but then she gave me a lamp and a long cord. I made a pillow out of a coat I grew out of. It's really cozy and the perfect place to hide my diaries from my nosy little brother and sister. Not that Raymond would care, but Opal would love to get her hands on my secrets and tell all of her friends. Maybe someday my daughter will read them. And then I can tell her all about the boy I met at church today! His name is John Wolf. He is nineteen and a college student. Bess and I have absolutely dissected him. Does that sound awful? What I mean is, we decided he has Bing Crosby eyes, Clark Gable hair and chin dimple, and the most beautiful Jimmy Stewart smile. He is tall, over six feet for sure, and he has a German accent. His father just started teaching at the college and they bought Mrs. Simpson's house on Clark Street. John didn't say anything about his mother, and I was too afraid to ask. What if something terrible happened to her? Maybe she ran off and left to become a movie star, or maybe something worse. Maybe she was murdered. There goes that wild imagination Mama says will get me in trouble someday.

I suppose it sounds horrid that I'm so fascinated by another boy, especially when Richard has promised to think of nothing and no one but me while he's at his grandparents' farm. I imagine people will talk, and he will hear all sorts of rumors. Maybe it was also wrong that I was glad I was wearing my navy dress with the white polka dots and that Bess had let me borrow her Tangee lipstick. I put a little on my cheeks too. I think I look way older with lipstick. Mama gave me "the look" but she didn't say "Not until you're sixteen!" like she usually does. Less than four months until lipstick and nylons! Anyway, back to John. He was impressed that I knew some German words. When I told him my great-great-grandparents came here from Germany a hundred years ago, he thought that was really something. His English is good, but his accent is so strong that I wanted to ask if he was born here or in Germany, but I didn't. He only lives five blocks from me so it wouldn't be all that strange if I happened to ride my bicycle past his house this week, would it? I just want to hear more about who he is and where he's been.

Guess I should write about other things too. I watched the pastor's two-year-old granddaughter during a church meeting last night, so now I have $18.45 toward my dreamy RCA phonograph. I stare at it in the window every time I walk past Gamble's. It is the most beautiful thing I have ever, ever seen, an RCA Victor Special, made of chrome and *aluminum and lined with red velvet. It latches and has a red handle for carrying it. Sometimes I feel like it's wrong to save for something that isn't a necessity when times are hard, but aren't music and beauty necessary when the days are bleak? Mother will probably need to borrow my money for groceries again, but I will keep saving until I'm thirty if I must.*

It was our turn to host Sunday dinner today and Grandpa teased Mama and me about making deviled chicken and devil's food cake on the Lord's Day. It was pretty funny. Everybody said my cake turned out perfect. The key to making it red is the boiling water. I made that cooked pecan frosting and it didn't sugar this time. Do I sound like I'm bragging? I guess I am. Suppose I better repent because our sermon this morning was all about being humble.

Good night, dear diary!

Chapter Three

Amy woke to a quiet house on Sunday morning. A rare treat. Tiptoeing around the kitchen, she filled the electric roaster oven with the pork ribs she'd prepped last night. They'd be fork tender and ready to finish off on the grill when church was over.

After a quick shower, she wrapped her hair in a towel and went out to the porch with her Bible and a cup of coffee sweetened with coconut sugar. She sat on the porch swing she'd found two blocks over at the end of a driveway on trash day. A few screws, new chains, and two coats of paint had created her favorite spot for time alone with the Lord. Or reading to the kids.

A slight breeze teased of much-needed rain. Though she didn't mind not having to mow the lawn the past two weeks, she longed to see green again. It was too early in the summer for grass that Jana described as "crunchy and prickly."

They'd lived in the house since May, but she still had to pinch herself every morning when she opened her eyes and stared up at the slanted bedroom ceiling in her one-hundred-and-twelve-year-old home. It needed work, but it was hers. Theirs.

She opened her Bible to the bookmarked page. Her gaze landed on the last verse of Psalm 27. "Wait for the Lord; be strong and take heart and wait for the Lord." She'd read the words on Friday and decided to memorize them and repeat them daily.

The screen door squeaked, and a sleepy Jana walked out, purple purse slung over the shoulder of her Elsa pajamas. She scrambled onto the swing, and Amy wrapped her arm around her. She smelled of lemon verbena shampoo. "Any dreams, pumpkin?"

Jana nodded. "I was wearing a sparkly dress and riding on a white horse on the carousel."

Amy couldn't tell from her tone of voice if it was a good dream or a "yucky" one. Two months ago, the happy dreams had started to outnumber the scary ones, but then they'd had a setback. The bad dreams started up again when she told the kids they'd be hearing a final answer about their adoption soon. Jana had asked in a trembling voice, "But maybe we can't stay with you, and we have to go back?"

Redirecting her thoughts, Amy said, "Riding the carousel sounds like fun." She'd taken the kids to Faust Park to ride the carousel soon after they moved, but Jana had been too afraid. "Should we go back to the park?"

Jana shook her head. "One of the horses in my dream was big and black and had giant teeth."

Amy pulled her closer, wondering, not for the first time, if a biological mother would have words in these times when she had no idea what to say. Jana's dreams were all different, but most involved a happy time interrupted by something scary. Monsters, dragons, wild animals… What did they mean? At least now Jana felt safe enough to talk about them. For the first few weeks, Matt was the only one who could comfort her, so Amy had let them share a room.

It was a big step for Jana when she decided she wanted her own room in their "new old" house.

"Is your room clean? All the cousins are coming for lunch today." Sometimes distraction was the only answer to the melancholy brought on by the "yucky" dreams.

"I jus' have to put all my lovies on the bed." Jana had recently counted her "lovies." Seventeen dolls and stuffed animals got assigned to a place on the floor surrounding her bed every night and carefully arranged on her Frozen bedspread every morning. "Are we having a picnic?"

"Yep. Barbeque, baked beans, and blackberry dumplings."

Jana giggled. "That's a lot of *B* words."

"Barbeque, baked beans, blackberry dumplings. Say that ten times real fast."

Jana tried, shoulders shaking with laughter. Music to Amy's ears. "Aunt Tracy is bringing that potato salad you love. Anna is bringing watermelon, and Sara said she made three-bean salad." When Jana stuck out her tongue, Amy laughed. "You can eat the green beans and give me the rest. And guess the very best part. Kevin is bringing all the stuff we need to make homemade ice cream."

"*Make* ice cream?" Jana's freckled nose crinkled.

"Yep. He'll bring—"

"Ice cream?" Matt's sleepy voice came through the screen door. He joined them on the swing. He'd slept in basketball shorts and no shirt. Amy tousled his messy hair and enlarged her one-armed hug to include her summer-tanned boy as she explained the process of making old-fashioned homemade ice cream.

When she finished, two pairs of eyes stared at her like she'd just promised a trip to Mars. These two had seen and heard things children shouldn't even be aware of, and yet were occasionally like wide-eyed toddlers experiencing the simple joys in life for the first time.

Matt squinted up at the century-old, gnarled red oak that would shade the entire west side of the house by the time of the picnic. A smile split his face. "It's gonna be a good day, Mom. A real good day."

The aroma of pork ribs simmering with onions, garlic, and honey barbeque sauce filled the house when they walked in from church, causing Amy's stomach to rumble so loud it made Jana laugh. After changing clothes, the kids joined her outside. Sunday dinners, a tradition started at least three generations earlier, were usually held at Jeff and Tracy's. Since Jeff was in the middle of a refinishing project that coated the first floor in dust, Amy had offered to host.

Amy lit the grill, and Jana helped her put the red and white checkered cloth on the picnic table. They'd just gotten it fastened down with metal clips when the first car pulled in. Tracy and Robin had promised to come early to help set up. Kai hauled lawn chairs from the trunk of Robin's Toyota then went to join Matt shooting baskets in the driveway.

As soon as Tracy, Robin, and Aunt Ruth, Robin's mother, had arranged their covered dishes on the table and gotten their glasses of iced tea, Tracy pulled something from her back pocket and motioned for them to sit at the picnic table. "It was all I could do to not show you this in church." She laid the paper in front of them.

Amy leaned closer. A black-and-white copy of the front page of the *Canton Press-News Journal* dated Thursday, May 21, 1987.

Tracy tapped on a notice in the middle of the paper, next to an announcement welcoming new members to the Chamber of Commerce.

No Suspects Yet

Police are still investigating the theft of a painting reported by former Canton resident Elizabeth Blair on Thursday, May 7. Miss Blair was visiting Mrs. Pearl Allen (widow of the late Howard Allen) when the three-foot by four-foot painting of a young woman disappeared from the Allen residence sometime between the hours of 10 p.m. Wednesday, May 6 and 6 a.m. Thursday the 7th. According to Mrs. Allen, the painting was a family heirloom, but held no significant monetary value. No photographs of the painting were available. Anyone with any information that may lead to the recovery of the painting and apprehension of the thief should contact Canton police or the Press-News.

"Wait. No photographs?" Aunt Ruth's eyebrows shot up. "There are dozens of pictures that were taken in front of the family room fireplace. You can see at least part of your Green Girl in all of them. Why wouldn't Mom give them a picture?" She sighed. "And why did Elizabeth report it? Why didn't Mom?"

"What else do you remember about the theft?" Robin asked. "Were they awake? Did they hear or see anything?"

Aunt Ruth took a moment to answer. "I remember Elizabeth being much more upset than Mom. They'd gotten into a fight, and she left earlier than she'd planned. That wasn't all that unusual, and I don't know that it had anything to do with the break-in. Elizabeth was a…difficult person. Mom acted like it was no big deal that someone broke into her house. She said it was time for a change of decor anyway, and she hung that landscape picture."

Amy picked up the clipping and read it again. "Do you remember anything else?"

"I was so busy keeping up with my eleven-year-old tomboy, I really didn't pay all that much attention, I guess."

Amy pulled her phone out of her pocket and scrolled to her notes app. "Let's start writing down all of our questions." She typed *Green Girl Mystery* at the top then wrote a few comments about the newspaper article.

Aunt Ruth sighed. "Why did we pick July for a three-week vacation? I don't want to leave all the mystery fun. You won't even be able to reach me by phone while we're in the Alaskan wilderness."

Robin plucked a potato chip from an overflowing bowl. "We'll catch you up on everything when you get back to civilization."

"I've got some news too." Amy told them about her conversation with Indiana, mentioning the man who was there asking about the painting just an hour before she arrived.

Tracy grimaced. "Creepy."

"You're sure we didn't tell Indiana where we live?" Robin asked.

"Pretty sure. And you gave him cash and didn't ask for a receipt, so I don't think there's any way we can be traced."

Robin wiped the condensation off her glass. "Except for the small matter of a map of Canton on the back of the painting." She pulled out her phone and showed her mother a picture of the map then turned it to face Tracy and Amy.

Three stars marked three lots on a rough grid of Canton. Tracy pointed to one of the stars. "That could be our house."

Robin nodded. "Gave me the willies when I realized that. But someone would really have to study it or know the town like we do to figure it out."

Amy agreed, but her pulse quickened as she realized that the man who asked Indiana about Green Girl may have seen the map on the back. Maybe it was the map, and not the painting, he'd wanted.

"This one"—Robin pointed to a star about two blocks from Grandma's house—"is that big redbrick house on Clark Street."

"The other one would be on the corner of Eighth and Lewis." Amy smoothed her right brow where a headache was starting. "Send this to me. I'll make a shared file we can all add to. Speaking of that…" Grateful for a change of subject, she showed the others a picture on her phone. "This is the maker's mark on the bottom of a mug made by the woman who sold Green Girl to Indiana. She's a student at Culver-Stockton."

"Seriously?" Tracy rubbed her arms, even though she couldn't possibly be chilled. "This is getting weirder by the minute. We find the painting two and a half hours away, sold by someone who went to school just blocks from where we live?"

Amy shrugged. "Indiana would call that a coinkydink."

"Grandma Pearl would call it a Godincidence." Tracy squinted at Amy's screen. "NC. Wonder what it stands for. Her initials?"

"Or the name of her business," Robin said.

"Could be either," Tracy said. "I'll show it to Jeff. Maybe he can ask around campus."

"I'll talk to Claire," Robin said. "She knows a ton of people on staff at CSC. Maybe she's got a connection in the art department."

Tracy drained her glass. "Grace said she'd keep searching archives for anything more about the robbery." Grace Park, one of Tracy's close friends, was the head librarian at the Brown Memorial Library. "She also suggested we talk to Columbia Burke."

Aunt Ruth laughed. "She was our *original* gossip columnist." She nudged Tracy's arm. The good-natured teasing about Tracy's job description was an endless source of family entertainment. "Columbia Burke is a hoot. And she didn't like her journalism referred to as gossip either."

Tracy nodded. "Grandma loved talking to her and said she could never have a better next-door neighbor, but Mom thought she was just a busybody and never told her anything. She didn't like the idea that I was following in her footsteps."

Amy smiled. "And now you get paid for being a busybody."

"It's not a job if you love what you do." Tracy pointed to Amy's phone. "We need to decide who's doing what. Robin, you talk to Claire, then maybe we make an appointment for all of us to talk to whoever she suggests at the college. I'll follow up with Grace, and I think we should all meet together with Columbia. Anything else?"

"That should cover it." Amy hopped up to turn the ribs just as Tracy's daughter and her family arrived. Sara got out of the passenger side, opened the back door, and lifted Zoe from her car seat. Tracy hurried to help, stretching her arms out for her sleeping granddaughter. Just a few minutes later Chad and Anna arrived with Corbin and Emerson.

Ignoring the familiar pinch in her chest, Amy tightened her grip on the tongs and focused on the task at hand. God alone knew if she would ever hold her own grandchild. Just then, two arms wrapped around her waist. "Look at my hair, Mom! I did it myself!" Jana stepped back and twirled in a circle, her ponytail, fastened with a glittery pink scrunchy, circling like helicopter blades.

The twinge just above her heart eased, replaced by a different kind of pressure that filled her whole chest. "I love it, sweetie." *And I love you.*

Chapter Four

At noon on Monday, Amy set a paper plate of potato salad and reheated ribs on the end of her kitchen table that wasn't covered with books and papers and the maps she'd bought from Indiana. Lunch alone. Something she'd never really appreciated before eight months ago.

Joining the church's Mom2Mom group in May was one of the best decisions she'd ever made. By the second meeting, Amy had bonded with two other foster mothers, set up weekly playdates, and found the perfect babysitter, Olivia, the fifteen-year-old daughter of one of them. Between the three moms, they had two ten-year-old boys, and girls that were seven, six, and five. Today, they were all enjoying a water balloon and pizza party at a house two blocks away, giving Amy three hours of quiet in which to make plans for a new first-grade class in a new school.

She looked down at the three boxes she'd pulled out of her closet. Textbooks, markers, bulletin board displays for every season, and twenty-four years of lesson planners. Twenty-four years. She would be forty-nine on July 31. She heaved a loud sigh as it dawned on her that she'd spent half of her life teaching.

So why did this year feel like her first? Twenty-four years ago, she started teaching in Steelville, three hours south of Canton, as a fill-in. The town known as "The Floating Capitol of the World," because vacationers flocked there every summer for tubing on the Huzzah and Meramec Rivers, offered everything she thought she needed. The small-town feel she'd grown up with, the beauty of nature, a bit of independence, and an escape from memories after her parents' tragic death.

Within a few weeks, she'd realized that memories follow wherever you go, and grieving wasn't something to be done alone. She couldn't count how many times she'd driven back to Canton for a weekend. And yet, by the end of that first year, when Steelville Elementary offered her a permanent position, she accepted. Five years later, she bought a three-bedroom house built before the Civil War. She rented the extra bedrooms to other teachers, six in all over the years. In another series of events Grandma Pearl labeled "Godincidences," the last two got married, one in August, the other in October the previous year, leaving her with two empty rooms right when she was ready for the foster-care home study.

The "home" feeling she'd had in Steelville lasted until six months ago, when she knew she didn't want to raise her children without the advice, support, and shared history of family. She'd worried that moving Matt and Jana to a different county might pose a problem, but since she'd offered to transport them to parental visits, she'd gotten a green light from the Crawford County Social Services office.

Leaving friends and the familiar work environment was one of the hardest things she'd ever done. Starting at a new school would be another one.

She had a forkful of Tracy's famous potato salad an inch from her mouth when her phone buzzed. At the sight of the name on the screen, her pulse skipped a couple of beats and she fumbled to answer.

"Hi, Amy." Melanie, Matt and Jana's social worker, always sounded a bit breathless. With Melanie's never-ending caseload, Amy understood why. "Just a quick call to say I don't have any updates. I know this is stressful. Wish I had something to tell you."

Amy repressed her sigh and tried to reassure herself that no news was good news. Or at least it wasn't bad. "I suppose I can't ask what's going on."

"To be honest, I'm not even sure. I know all concerned parties are in communication with each other. Hopefully they'll come to the right conclusion soon."

From the beginning, Melanie hadn't hidden her opinion that Matt and Jana should stay with Amy.

"Okay. Thanks for the update. Or non-update, I guess."

"Hang in there. I'll call as soon as I know something."

Tension that was becoming all too common began to build at the base of Amy's skull. She picked up her fork, then set it down when her phone buzzed again. Robin's name flashed on the screen.

Had God prompted her cousin to call just at the exact moment she needed a family connection? "Hi, Robin."

"Hi. Did you wake up with a food hangover like me? My fingers are so puffy I can't even get my rings on. But those ribs were so, so delicious."

"Thank you. Grandma's recipes come through every time. I hear you on the puffiness. I drank about a gallon of water this morning. What's up?"

"Claire called back. She said we should talk to Professor Arthur Douglas. He teaches studio art. Claire thought he'd be the most likely to know the woman who sold Green Girl to Indiana Jones. Do you want to set up an appointment? Hayley can handle things here at the store so I can be free anytime."

They chitchatted for a few minutes, until the bell over the shop door at Pearls of Wisdom dinged in the background, announcing a customer's arrival. "Go sell some expensive antiques," Amy said. "I'll call the college."

Amy finished relishing the fall-off-the-bone ribs made from a recipe that had been handed down for generations, then she washed the barbecue sauce off her face and hands and called Culver-Stockton College. When she was transferred to the art department, she talked to a secretary who said Professor Douglas had an opening at two. Amy glanced at the clock above the sink. She hadn't expected to get an appointment today, but she'd make it work. When she got off the phone, she made another call to ensure Olivia could watch the kids, then contacted Tracy and Robin.

When she hung up, her thoughts reverted to Melanie's call.

With a heavy sigh, Amy opened her laptop to search for a spreadsheet. The words that greeted her when the screen came to life made her smile. Exactly what she needed at that moment. *Wait for the Lord; be strong and take heart and wait for the Lord.*

They'd arrived fifteen minutes before their appointment, so the women sat at a picnic table on the beautifully manicured grounds of Culver-Stockton College, surrounded by historic redbrick buildings.

Several groups of students congregated at picnic tables or on the grass. The campus had a more casual feel during summer sessions when the population shrank.

"This is the best place for people watching," Tracy said between bites of a sandwich. She'd opted for a later lunch break today so she wouldn't miss out on the appointment. "I spent a lot of hours here before kids, waiting to have lunch with Jeff."

"Speaking of...did you show him the maker's mark?" Robin asked.

"Yep. He had no idea who NC might be. Though, as we all know, he can be the stereotypical absentminded professor. He does know Professor Douglas and has a lot of respect for him."

"Good to know." Amy nodded toward a group of young women in shorts and T-shirts sitting in a circle on the grass...grass that clearly got watered more than hers. Nothing "crunchy and prickly" in sight. "Were we ever that young?"

Robin gave a wistful sigh. "Seems like a long time ago. In five years, I'll have a college kid of my own."

"The dreaded empty-nest years," Tracy said, teasing in her voice. And then she glanced at Amy and quickly looked down at the notebook in front of her. "So what's our game plan?"

"First," Amy said, "I'll show him the maker's mark and ask if he knows..." Amy stared at a blond woman standing up from the circle of students. "Look at her shirt!" she whispered.

The front of the young woman's aqua shirt displayed a dragonfly. And the letters *NC*.

The woman headed toward one of the residence halls, and Amy stood. "I'm going to follow her."

Tracy tugged the hem of Amy's capri pants. "We're going with you."

Robin and Tracy stood and the three began power walking to catch up to the young woman with a backpack slung over one shoulder. "What are you going to say?" Robin asked, directing her question at Amy.

"No clue." They were about ten feet behind her. "Miss?" Was that even politically correct these days? "Excuse me."

The young woman stopped. "Yes?"

"I noticed your shirt. I saw the same symbol on a mug a friend of mine had. Are you the artist?"

The young woman glanced down, as if she couldn't remember what she'd put on this morning. "Oh. No. I borrowed this from my roommate. Not sure where she got it." She shrugged. "Have to get to class." She turned and sprinted away from them.

Amy's shoulders dropped. "She didn't give me time to ask who her roommate is."

Tracy tipped her head toward the Herrick Center building. "Let's go talk to the professor."

As Robin reached for the door handle, a tall, bald young man and a redheaded woman in her early twenties walked out. "Wait!" Robin said.

They turned around. The woman was wearing a pink T-shirt. With the dragonfly logo on the front.

"Hi!" Robin raised a hand in awkward greeting. "I just noticed your shirt. Did you design it?"

"Nope." She shot a questioning look at the young man. "Why?"

"I really like the artist. Do you know her?"

"Nope. Some girl was selling them." Her fingers fluttered against her tablet.

"Do you know her name?"

The young man put his arm protectively around the woman and took a step back. "We don't know her." With quick strides, they walked away.

Arthur Douglas's office was on the first floor. Just before they reached it, Amy held up a hand. "Let's keep it simple. Just ask him about the maker's mark and not mention the painting."

Her sister and cousin sent her curious looks.

Amy shrugged. "Just a weird feeling. Intuition, maybe. Or overactive imagination. Let's just be a little cautious."

Tracy gave her a thumbs-up. "Good thinking."

The office door was halfway open. Robin rapped lightly.

"Come in."

The man behind the desk, his hair graying at the temples, wore a blue oxford shirt with the sleeves rolled back. He stood when they walked in and offered his hand to each of them as they introduced themselves. Then he motioned for them to take the three chairs in front of his desk.

While Robin explained they were looking for an art student who made pottery, Amy scanned the small space. One large window framed two of the beautiful historic buildings. A long, low bookcase behind the professor was crammed with books and files. Several paint canvases leaned against the shelf. The desk was appropriately messy for an art professor. Directly in front of Amy sat a stack of books. The one on top was entitled *Goring's Man in Paris: The Story of a Nazi Art Plunderer and His World*. The spine on the one below it read *The Monuments Men*. A still-life painting on one wall was signed *A. Douglas*.

"Yes, I know her." Professor Douglas rubbed his chin as he looked at the dragonfly logo on Robin's phone. "Her name is Niesha Carter. Very talented young artist." His brow furrowed as he handed the phone back. "Do you know where she is?"

Robin shot a quick glance at Amy. All Robin had told him was that they were interested in finding out more about the artist because they admired her work.

Amy felt prickles on the back of her neck. "We were hoping you could tell us."

He shook his head. "I have no idea. She's one of our most diligent students. She was taking three classes this summer. Never missed one. Until last week. No one has seen her for over a week. One of my colleagues talked to her roommate. Her dorm room is completely cleared out. She didn't leave a note or contact any of her friends. It's like she just vanished into thin air."

September 19, 1937

Guess what? John saw the Hindenburg at the factory where it was built, and his father knew Count Ferdinand von Zeppelin, the man who invented the first zeppelin! Mr. Wolf lived in the same town as the count, who died before John was born. I could sit and listen to John's stories for hours. He said the Hindenburg was breathtaking and so much bigger than he had imagined from pictures. When they heard about the crash, his father cried.

Bess has a cold, so she stayed home from church today. After the service, John and I took a walk. Mom said we could only go around the block. I'm sure John thinks I'm such a child because I had to ask my mommy's permission. I know people will talk, but I don't really care. I just want to hear about all of his adventures. He's been to Paris! I wanted to hear all about the Eiffel Tower and Arc de Triomphe and French pastries, but he mostly likes to talk about artists and paintings. He finally told me a little about growing up in Germany. His mother died when he was ten. That's so sad. When I asked why they moved, he said it was because his father's brother lives in St. Louis and he invited them. I know there is much more to the story. There is something so wonderfully mysterious about him! Since Germany occupied the Rhineland last year, Grandpa has been saying there is going to be another big war. I hope that doesn't happen.

Anyway, back to small-town life in the US. Our church is having an ice cream social and pie auction next Sunday afternoon. I was sneaky. When I was asking John about Paris bakeries, I found out that rhubarb pie is his least favorite and he loves cream pie topped with blueberries. He was *surprised that I knew what cream pie was. Thanks, Grandma! The recipe is so simple: 3/4 cups sugar, two heaping tablespoons flour, two cups heavy cream, and two stiffly beaten egg whites. I'm going to bake a pie every day this week because my pie crust is good, but not as good as Grandma's yet. Hope I don't look like a zeppelin by Sunday!*

Good night, dear diary!

Chapter Five

Amy rested her cheek on Jana's freshly washed curls. They were snuggled together on the couch, both in pajamas, waiting for "Matt the server" to emerge from the kitchen with their giant popcorn bowl. "Lots of salt!" Jana yelled. Amy covered her ringing ear and laughed. To think this child had barely spoken above a whisper eight months ago.

"Not *too* much salt," Amy warned. Jana crossed her arms and huffed melodramatically. Another beautiful thing. She was not only understanding the joking that was part of the fabric of the Allen family, she was also taking part in it. Amy tapped her nose. "You're so cute when you're mad."

Matt padded across the old in-need-of-refinishing plank floor in his bare feet, carrying a plastic tub with MOVIE NIGHT! scrawled on the side in permanent marker. Originally filled with bags of microwave popcorn and several pounds of movie theater candy, it had been a gift from Robin the week the kids had come to live with Amy. Movie night was now an every-Monday tradition. Tonight, they were watching *The Stray*, and Amy braced herself for the "I want a puppy!" whines that were sure to follow this saga of a rescue dog.

She needn't have worried. The popcorn was only half gone and the movie half over when the dark and quiet setting after a day of sunshine, water, and pizza did its magic, and she had a sleeping child leaning on each shoulder. A little taste of heaven.

Moving as little as possible, she tapped her phone and texted Tracy and Robin. First, with a selfie that garnered lots of hearts and an "aww" emoji, then with a question. ANYBODY LOOK FOR NC ONLINE?

WHO HAS TIME FOR SOCIAL MEDIA? Robin quipped.

Tracy said, GUESS I'M A SLEUTHING FLUNKY.

Amy answered with, CAN'T DO ANYTHING ELSE AT THE MOMENT, SO I'M GOING TO SEE WHAT I CAN FIND.

YOU KNOW, YOU CAN SEND THEM TO BED. This from Tracy, accompanied by a kissing wink.

Amy smiled and gave a two-word reply. NO WAY.

It only took a few taps to find Niesha Carter on Facebook. The young Black woman was beautiful. Flawless skin the color of café au lait, tight, dark ringlets hanging to her shoulders, and lovely, almond-shaped eyes. Amy took a screenshot and sent it to her sleuthing buddies, then started reading through Niesha's posts. After ten minutes, she'd learned very little. Most of her posts were art related. Amy could see she was talented, and dedicated to her craft, but didn't she have a social life? Amy tapped on *Photos* and scrolled through hundreds of pictures of pottery and paintings. And then…one of a group of students, all wearing dragonfly shirts. In the middle, next to Niesha, stood the redhead who'd said she'd bought her T-shirt from "some girl."

She sent the photo to Tracy and Robin, then clicked on Niesha's *About* page and read through a very brief bio. *Works at NC*

Designs. Studies at Culver-Stockton College. Lives in Canton, MO. In a relationship.

"Not helpful," Amy whispered. She tapped back to *Photos*, searching for anything that could provide more information. She stopped at a picture of Niesha with a tall, husky man. Midtwenties, probably. Buzzed hair, week-old beard, pale skin, and *NC* tattooed on his forearm. In contrast to Niesha's strappy black dress and classy, sparkly earrings, he wore faded jeans and a flannel shirt with the cuffs rolled back and a tear on one shoulder. "Opposites attract, I guess," Amy mused.

Niesha's last post was dated June 22. Nineteen days ago.

"What if she was kidnapped?" Amy sat on the floor in Grandma's attic late on Tuesday afternoon, distracted from sorting pictures by the question of what had happened to Niesha Carter. Matt and Jana were on the opposite end of the room. Matt had spent the first hour curled on a pile of old quilts reading a Percy Jackson book with Sadie, Jeff and Tracy's goldendoodle, at his feet, but he was now using the cracks between floorboards as a drag strip for the marbles he'd found in a moth-eaten cloth bag in a cardboard box. Jana played with a family of wooden dolls that Grandma Pearl had likely enjoyed when she was Jana's age.

Tracy, perched on a wooden box while sorting through old record albums, laughed. "Imaginating much?"

The word from their childhood sparked a smile. In the midst of playing house or putting on a puppet show, Amy had often told her sister and cousin they needed to "imaginate" better.

"Although," Tracy continued, "the bald guy with the redhead did seem a bit skittish, like he was afraid we'd ask more questions."

Amy ran a hand through hair that had a mind of its own in the heat of the attic. "I thought so too. She could have left school for any number of reasons. Maybe she ran out of money, or had a fight with her boyfriend, but she disappeared right after she passed Green Girl off to Indiana like a hot potato, and he said there was definitely something strange going on. And who is the guy who was looking for it right before I showed up at the flea market?" She rubbed her temples. "I wish I'd had the presence of mind to ask what the guy looked like. We don't even have a clue how old he is. Maybe Niesha's grandfather stole the painting from Grandma. But then why would Niesha be getting rid of it?"

Tracy pulled her phone out of her pocket. "There must be a way to get in touch with someone from the flea market. Maybe we can find out Indiana's real name and contact info." She tapped and scrolled then smiled. "There's a form to fill out and someone will get back to us. I'm putting in your number since Indiana will remember you."

"Okay." Needing to give her brain a break, Amy picked up a stack of pictures. The task was daunting. While Grandma Pearl had dozens of organized photo albums filled with select images, one for each year until 2001, she had also kept every single photograph she had ever taken, going back to the 1930s, plus a few precious ambrotypes and tintypes from the mid-1800s. The pictures were jumbled in shoe boxes in no particular order, which meant each time Amy reached into a box, she didn't know what decade she'd be transported to.

Because of her love for history, Amy had been unanimously elected for the job. Though she was thoroughly enjoying it, she hadn't been prepared for the scope of the task. Organizing the thousands of photos Grandma had deemed not album-worthy would probably take her at least a year. The one saving grace in this task was that Grandma had meticulously written names and dates on every single photo.

The box she was currently sorting held snapshots from the 1960s and '70s with a few '80s thrown in. She laughed at a picture of Grandma in her forties, dressed like Dorothy from *The Wizard of Oz*. Braids, white blouse, blue-and-white-checked pinafore. Grandpa stood on one side of her, wearing a costume that appeared to be made of coffee cans. On her other side was a man dressed as the scarecrow. Turning it over, she read *With JW at church harvest party, 1969.*

She picked up a photo of baby Tracy sitting on Grandma's lap. She handed the picture to Tracy.

"Aww. I was so cute."

"You look a lot like Grandma now that you're old." Amy grinned and winked. "Thankfully, perms went out of fashion long before your fifties." She held up a photograph of a tightly permed Grandma Pearl blowing out candles on her a cake with 65 written on it in bright blue frosting.

They were silent for the next few minutes, Tracy cleaning and sorting record albums by decade, and Amy doing the same with loose photographs. Occasionally, she held up one that evoked a memory or gave them a glimpse of Grandma's life before they were born. Vacations, family dinners, holidays. And then she found another shot of Grandma's sixty-fifth birthday party, taken on December 21, 1986, the same day as the earlier one. Since Grandma's birthday was on Christmas Day, she rarely had a party on her actual birthday. Five women stood in front of the fireplace with Grandma, who was wearing a crown. "Who are these people? There are only initials on the back. C, D, A, P, E, R." She gave the picture to Tracy.

"The one on the left is Columbia, but she's so young there, I'm not surprised you didn't recognize her. By the way, I called and left her a message yesterday." Tracy pointed. "I think the blond on Grandma's left is Elizabeth Blair."

"Recognize anyone else?"

Tracy squinted. "I think the young one next to Columbia might be Debra Smith."

"The owner of the Canton Art Gallery?"

"Yeah. Her mom was one of Grandma's close friends, so maybe A or R is Debra's mom." Tracy handed the photo back to Amy. "If we take this much time with each one, we'll never get to organizing our own pictures and our grandkids will be stuck doing the same thing."

Amy nodded. "And most of ours are digital. They'll probably hate having to deal with the ancient iPhone 13 technology."

As she slid the birthday party picture into a zipper bag labeled *1980s*, she took a second glance and pulled it out. "Look. You can see three-fourths of Green Girl in this, and we've got tons of pictures where you can see all of it."

"So why in the world wouldn't Grandma have given one to the police?"

Amy sighed. "Just one of way too many questions. At what point do we decide to quit chasing rabbit trails and give up on this quest?"

Tracy shook her head and was about to say something when her phone rang. After a short conversation, she hung up. "Well, we're not giving up yet. Lunch with Columbia at noon tomorrow."

Columbia Burke still lived next door to Grandma's house in a craftsman-style house built in 1923 from a Sears & Roebuck kit. Framed on her dining room wall was the original floorplan diagram in an advertisement for "The Bandon," with a base price of $3,176.

From her seat at the end of a cherry dining table polished to a mirror shine, Columbia smiled at her guests and nodded to her *temporary* housekeeper to serve lunch. Amy had a feeling "housekeeper" was a title Columbia chose for the woman who was probably hired to care for her more than the house. In her late seventies, she had undergone her second hip replacement six weeks earlier. By stressing that Hilda was only going to be with her for another week, she made it clear that she hated how the surgeries had interfered with her independence.

Robin commented on the crown molding and asked Columbia how she'd managed to maintain the house's historical charm.

"Charles and I moved here with three children and two dogs in 1974. The previous owners painted all the woodwork, and Charles spent most of his evenings and weekends for about five years restoring it back to the original."

"Five years?" Tracy's voice squeaked.

Columbia laughed. "It always takes longer than you think it will. My best advice is something Charles said often: 'One room at a time. One step at a time.' If you look at the whole project, it will only serve to discourage you."

"I think I'll have a plaque made with that quote." Tracy thanked Hilda for a plate of puff pastry filled with chicken salad and garnished with fresh fruit, then turned back to Columbia. "Were you working at the paper before you moved here?"

"Yes. We were married here in Canton and rented a house for the first few years. I started at the paper in 1968. I was home with two little ones and another on the way, and even though I loved motherhood, I felt like my college education was just going to waste. Plus we were saving to buy a house. I'd seen a 'Comings and Goings' column in a newspaper when we were vacationing in South Carolina, and it just seemed like something Canton needed. I presented it as a way to pull the community together, but the editor agreed to it because 'gossip sells.'" Her barely wrinkled skin crinkled around her eyes when she laughed. "I was a bit, shall we say, 'aggressive' back then. Not everyone appreciated being peppered with questions about who they had for dinner and what they did on vacation, but I had many loyal contributors to my Cantonbury Tales column. Your grandmother was one of them."

Tracy nodded. "I remember reading all the details about one of our family Christmas gatherings in your column. Made me feel like a celebrity."

Columbia took a sip from a glass of water garnished with a strawberry and a slice of lemon. "Pearl and I had many conversations about the morality of what I did. My 'nose for news' may have made me a bit annoying, but I only reported firsthand stories."

Hilda set a plate in front of Columbia, who thanked her then said, "Let's pray." After a simple prayer of thanks, she addressed Tracy again. "You mentioned on the phone that you had some questions. How can I help? And, by the way, I've had every single column I ever wrote digitized and filed by date, so I should be able to put my fingers on just about anything you might want. You can also access them on the library's website."

"That's wonderful. What we're looking for is anything you can tell us about the painting that was stolen from Grandma's house on May 6 or 7 of 1987."

Columbia's fork stopped halfway to her mouth, and she set it down again. She picked up her glass, took two sips, then slowly shook her head. "I'm sorry. I can't help you there." Parallel lines formed between her dark eyes. "I never knew what I did to offend her, but I could tell the moment Pearl heard my voice that she was not pleased with me. It was maybe a week and a half after the theft was reported in the paper. She'd been acting strange, canceling things and avoiding people since it happened. I asked if she had any intuition about who took it or details that could help townspeople be on the lookout for suspects. She said everyone was making way too big a deal out of one old painting gone missing and if one more person asked her about it she was going to scream."

"Grandma said that?" Tracy asked. "That's so unlike her."

"I know. I've wondered since if she was far more traumatized by the break-in than anyone knew." Columbia looked down at her manicured nails. "It was the only time I felt completely shut out of Pearl's life."

Chapter Six

*T*racy brought out frosted glasses of sweet tea, and they sat at Grandma Pearl's Eastlake dining room table, talking about their visit with Columbia.

"Interesting that she mentioned Grandma saying the theft was no big deal," Robin said. "I get that the painting might not have been worth much monetarily, but someone invading your personal space while you're sleeping is definitely not nothing."

Tracy nodded. "It's like she wanted to divert everyone's attention from it."

Amy curled the corner of her napkin, then watched it unroll as a memory played out in her mind. "Do you remember Grandma's response when Bobby Carson stole my bike in fourth grade? I knew he had it and I was ready to charge over to his house and take it back and tell his parents they'd better ground him for life."

"I remember." Tracy smiled. "Grandma made you bake cookies for him."

"What?" Robin looked from Amy to Tracy. "I don't think I've heard this."

Amy closed her eyes for a moment, reliving the day. "Grandma sat me down and told me about Bobby's mother raising four children by herself. Her husband had left them, and she was cleaning houses to keep food on the table. There was no money left for extras like bicycles."

"I can still hear you arguing with her," Tracy said.

"Oh yeah. My righteous nine-year-old indignation came out in full force. Stealing was wrong, no matter what the reason, and that boy needed to pay for his sins." Amy laughed. "Grandma said she'd go over to their house with me, but first we needed to bake cookies for them. I remember slamming cupboard doors and smacking balls of cookie dough on the pan like I was throwing rocks at Bobby. When they were done, we boxed up a couple dozen and walked to the Carsons' house. On the way, she told me not to say a word about my bike."

Robin raised one eyebrow. "I can imagine how you responded."

"Yeah. It wasn't pretty. But she quoted from Romans 12 about feeding your enemies and told me to pray for them and wait and see what happened."

Robin leaned in. "And?"

"And we had a nice, polite visit. Mrs. Carson thanked us profusely. Bobby didn't say a word, just sat there stuffing his face with cookies. I was steaming as we left, ready to blast Grandma about the injustice and foolishness of not confronting Bobby, but we were a block away when he came flying up on my bike and said he was sorry. And then I did something that shocked me as much as it did Grandma. I said, 'I forgive you, and if you ever want to borrow it, just ask.'"

"Wow. Talk about a life lesson. I can think of times I could use that with Kai. So…" Robin rested her chin on her fist. "You're saying it wouldn't be out of character at all for Grandma to have done the Romans 12 thing in this case, right? What if she knew who stole it and she was loving her enemy by not letting him or her get caught?"

Tracy nodded. "How often did we think we were going to get in big trouble for staying up all night when we slept over, or for polishing off a dozen of her homemade donuts for a midnight snack when our moms had said no sugar before bed. She never told on us unless it was something really bad. I can see her reaching out to the thief and telling him about Jesus rather than sending him to jail."

Just as Amy copied Tracy's nod, Matt crept around the corner, camera in hand. "Don't look now," Amy said in a stage whisper loud enough for him to hear, "but I think we have a foreign spy in our midst."

Matt came out from his hiding place behind the door. Pointing at his camouflage-print tank top and matching shorts, he gave a fake pout. "But I'm invisible." The women laughed.

"Hey!" Amy pointed at the camera. "Show us the video you took of Indiana Jones."

Matt's face glowed with pride as he searched for it. "I can hook this up to the TV so we can see it bigger."

"That would be great," Tracy said. "Do you know how..." He was gone before she could finish her question. "Evidently he does."

Amy barely had time for a sip of peach tea before Matt bounded back in. "C'mon. It's all set."

Carrying their glasses, they took seats, and Amy pulled Jana onto her lap. Matt had connected his video camera to the TV with an HDMI cord. "How do they know this stuff?" Robin whispered.

"And now"—Matt swooped his arm at the television like a carnival barker—"for the first time ever, a presentation of *moi* spying on Indiana Jones."

The video was surprisingly steady and the audio clearer than Amy would have expected, considering Matt had been hiding behind a lawn sculpture about six feet away.

It began with Indiana saying, "Guess I did say I sold it to three women who said it used to belong to their grandma. Probably shouldn't have said that. Just didn't think."

"Did you tell him anything else about us?" Amy asked.

"Nope," he answered. "That was it."

"Is there anything else you can tell me—"

"Stop!" Amy slid Jana off her lap and jumped up. "Pause it." Heart pounding, she walked closer to the screen.

"What is it?" Robin asked.

Amy pulled her phone out of her pocket, tapped to Facebook, and typed in *Niesha Carter,* then went to Niesha's photos. "Look." She held up the picture of Niesha and the burly man with the buzz cut. Then she pointed to the TV screen, at a man standing at the booth just behind Indiana's, gesturing in the general direction of the empty table once occupied by Niesha. Buzz cut. *NC* tattooed on his shoulder. "I don't know who he is, but Niesha knows him."

"Maybe he works at the flea market," Tracy said, her tone clearly trying to calm Amy's nerves.

Amy ignored the logical suggestion. "Or maybe he's her boyfriend."

Matt bounced on his toes. "So maybe I actually got something? I videoed a suspect?"

Amy rubbed the goose bumps on her arms then forced reason to take over. "A possible suspect. You did good work, buddy. It sure looks like there's a connection between Niesha and this man."

Amy plopped onto the love seat and crossed her arms, as if she could somehow protect herself from what she now knew but wouldn't say out loud in front of the kids.

The man, whoever he was, had been close enough to hear everything she'd said to Indiana.

After Robin left, Tracy turned to Amy with a familiar worried-big-sister look. "Stay for supper. We can get Jeff's input on all this. And you can spend the night if you want."

Amy felt her eyes widen as she stared back. "Do you think the kids and I are in danger?" What was Tracy thinking? There was no way the guy would know where they lived unless he'd followed them home on Saturday.

"No." Tracy's answer came a bit too quick. "You just seem upset."

Amy shook her head. "I'm fine." It wasn't completely true, but her thoughts hadn't gone where Tracy's apparently had. For once, she wasn't the one imagining. "But supper would be wonderful."

"Jeff's been dropping hints about how long it's been since I made toasted ravioli. It's an all-afternoon job, and I never feel like going through so much work just for the two of us. How's that sound for a distraction?"

"Perfectly delicious."

"I think I have everything...semolina flour, cheese, and more tomatoes than I know what to do with. Do you want to make pasta or sauce?"

"Pasta. I love using your ravioli wheel. Plus, it's a more thought-intensive job."

"Done. If the kids are okay, let's get started."

Amy checked on Matt and Jana. As usual, Matt had brought his book and was perfectly content curled in Jeff's recliner. Jana was playing with the dollhouse Jeff had made for Sara when she was Jana's age.

Tracy was in the garden when Amy returned to the kitchen. Her recipe card for toasted ravioli sat on the counter. Amy found the bag of flour in the pantry, took four eggs out of the refrigerator, cracked them into a glass bowl, then whisked them with salt and added half the flour. She incorporated the remaining semolina with a fork until it formed what the recipe passed down from Grandma Pearl termed a "shaggy" dough, then she sprinkled flour on the counter and dumped the dough on the dusted surface.

The recipe called for "vigorous" kneading. The perfect therapy for her mood. As she folded, pressed, and turned the dough over and over, she thought of Grandma's hands. How many loaves of bread and servings of pasta had she kneaded in her lifetime? "Best thing to do when you're mad at someone is make bread for them," she'd said more than once. Or cookies. "Love in action," Grandma called it. "You get out your frustrations and bless your enemy all at the same time."

Had she been talking about a particular enemy? Had she done what Robin called the "Romans 12 thing"—if your enemy is hungry, feed him—with the person who'd stolen the painting? It was easy to imagine her reaching out in love to someone who'd hurt or offended her.

The dough was beginning to feel smooth and elastic by the time Tracy walked in with a basket of tomatoes and a bundle of herbs.

Amy felt a swell of pride for this woman she was blessed to call sister. Tracy worked as a nurse for several years after completing her training, but chose to be a stay-at-home mom after Chad was born and then took on the part-time columnist job that perfectly fit her inquisitive nature.

As Tracy set the basket on the counter, Amy blurted, "I'm so glad you're my sister."

Tracy turned and tipped her head to one side. "I am too. But where did that come from?"

"I was just thinking of Grandma's hands and all the meals she made, and then you walk in carrying stuff from the garden just like she used to do in this very room, and I was thinking what an amazing mom you are and how I hope I can be half as good, and I'm so grateful for you." Surprised by the sting of tears, she looked down then quickly turned to the drawer next to her and pulled out the plastic wrap.

The next thing she knew, Tracy's arms were wrapped around her, triggering pent-up tears and blubbering that hardly made sense even to her. "I'm just so blessed with an amazing family and beautiful kids and an awesome house, and I should be enjoying all of it, but instead I'm anxious and scared about losing the kids—"

"Shh. Shh. Shh." Tracy patted her back. "'Take therefore no thought for the morrow: for the morrow shall take thought for the things of itself. Sufficient unto the day is the evil thereof.'" She quoted the verse from Matthew in the King James Version—the way Grandma had done so often when anxiety had gotten the best of her.

When her tears quieted, Amy pulled away and wiped her face with both hands. "Thank you. It used to be easier to follow that before I had to start believing it for three."

Tracy smiled. "Oh, believe me, I know. And I had time to ponder it as my kids grew up. You became three overnight, Little Mama. So cut yourself some slack and get back to the ravioli."

With a watery grin, Amy ripped off a piece of plastic wrap and snugly bundled her ball of dough.

If only she could protect the precious souls in her care as easily.

Chapter Seven

"What did Art say about the painting?" Jeff dipped another piece of toasted ravioli in thick marinara and popped it in his mouth.

Amy looked at Tracy, then back at Jeff. "We didn't tell him about it. We were just trying to find the student who sold it to Indiana Jones."

"Indiana Jones." Jeff smiled and shook his head. "You ladies do make life interesting." He stabbed a bite of salad. "Actually, Maura Childs is the art history professor. She's the one you should talk to about the painting. Pretty sure she's been at the college since it was founded."

"In 1853?" Tracy gave him a playful slap.

"Well, she might not be quite as old as dirt, but close. She could probably figure out when it was painted, maybe even tell who painted it if it was a local artist or someone famous. Your Green Girl has kind of a Renoir vibe. Maybe we're sitting on something that could let us hire professionals to finish the renos on both of our houses, pay off the mortgage on Robin's store, and take the whole family on a cruise."

Tracy sent him a mock glare. "Green Girl is not for sale. At any price."

Jana tipped her head to one side and asked, "Why does everyone call her a green girl? Just her dress is green. *She* isn't."

Matt laughed and pointed at Jana's striped sundress. "Wouldn't you like us to call you Pink and Purple Girl?"

Jana tucked her chin into her chest but couldn't hide her smile. "Yeah."

Amy gestured to Jana's empty plate. "Well, Pink and Purple Girl, if you would like to be excused, you can go play."

With a broad grin, Jana skipped out of the room.

"Can I go read?" Matt jumped up without waiting for an answer.

"Give your eyes a rest for a bit," Amy answered.

"Tell you what," Jeff said, "why don't you see if you can find a soccer ball in the garage, and I'll come out and show you some of my mean skills in a few minutes."

"All *right*!" Matt ran toward the door to the kitchen, then skidded to a stop and returned for his dirty plate. Turning to Tracy, he said, "Thank you for the food, Aunt Tracy. It was delicious."

Tracy gave him a hug. "And thank you for being an amazingly polite nephew."

When the kitchen screen door banged, Amy pressed her hand to her chest. "Thank you. Both of you. I can't imagine raising them without your support."

"And we'd be mad if you tried," Jeff said. "Now humor the history buff and fill me in on all of your investigative adventures."

Tracy recapped a few things she'd already told him, then Amy handed him her phone with a picture of Niesha.

Jeff stroked his chin. "She looks familiar, but she hasn't been in any of my classes."

When he handed the phone back, Amy found the group picture and pointed out the girl with the red hair who had pretended she didn't know Niesha.

"This one I know. Mandy…no, Mindy. Common last name. Jones, I think. Mindy Jones. She was in a summer class I taught on Missouri history three years ago. So she's probably going into her senior year."

Tracy patted his hand. "I knew I married you for a reason."

"Because I have a head full of generally useless information?"

"Yep."

Jeff blew her an air kiss. "Matt said something about filming a suspect."

Amy tried to keep the worry out of her voice as she told him about the video.

"Isn't it possible he was a vendor at the flea market? You have no proof this man and Niesha were close, other than one picture of the two of them. And the tattoo." Jeff's expression darkened with his last three words. "You haven't seen anything suspicious since Saturday?"

Amy shook her head. "Nothing. And I think I would have noticed if someone got off on the same exit and followed me to our neighborhood. I was pretty scared when I realized he could have been listening in on our conversation, but I think I can look at it a bit more rationally now. I don't think he followed me."

"You know you and the kids are welcome here anytime. If you have even the slightest concern…"

"I know." Amy took a slow breath. Jeff was making her edgy. "Thank you."

As if sensing the downward spiral of Amy's mood, Tracy flashed a brilliant smile. "Who's up for an Oreo flurry at Big O's? While the boys play ball, the girls will clean up, and then let's go indulge."

Tension seemed to flow from Amy's shoulders to her fingertips and then dissipate. Big O's Eats and Treats, with its mascot, a leather-jacketed pig sitting on a motorcycle and holding an ice cream cone, served up an array of sweet treats and true Southern barbecue. Going out for her favorite ice cream, such a simple, normal thing, grounded her back in reality. She was safe. Matt and Jana were safe. Surrounded by family and a tradition older than she was. She grinned at her sister. "I'm in."

On Thursday, Amy pulled up to Robin's antique shop, Pearls of Wisdom, with Matt in the back seat. They had an appointment with Professor Maura Childs. Tracy had happily volunteered to watch Corbin and Emerson so Anna could go to a doctor appointment, and she'd invited Jana to come over and play with them. "Matt too," she'd said, "if he wants to."

Not surprisingly, he didn't. "Can't I go spying with you?"

"We're not spying," Amy had replied. "We're doing research."

"Well, whatever you call it, can I come?"

Would her inability to say no to those puppy dog eyes land them both in trouble when he reached the teen years?

They got out of the car, and Matt pointed at two strands of pearls hanging on the black velvet jewelry display form in the front window. "Are those real?"

"You'll have to ask Robin." Amy tousled his hair. "You're starting to notice details and ask good questions. All good qualities for a super sleuth."

She was sure he grew an inch before her eyes, nourished by a sincere compliment. When he'd first come to live with her, affirmations seemed to trigger acting-out behavior, as if he needed to prove her wrong before he let himself start to believe it. From the little she knew of his life prior to getting in the system, she was sure he hadn't often been validated. It had taken more patience than she possessed without God's help to get them through those early months.

They walked through the door, and the bell above them announced their presence. Robin stood behind the counter talking on the phone. She smiled and held up one finger.

"Hey, Mom, look." Matt picked up a grayish-blue, speckled ceramic jar with a cork stopper. On the front was an ichthus, the Christian symbol of two intersecting arcs made to look like a fish. "Can I get this for the marbles I found in Grandma's attic?"

"How much is it?"

He turned the jar over. And they gasped in unison.

"What?" Robin walked over to them. "Is the price too high? We can always adjust for friends and family." Both brows rose as she stared at the bottom of the jar and the maker's mark.

NC, and a now familiar winged insect.

Half an hour before their appointment time, Amy, Robin, and Matt walked to the same place on campus where they'd seen the group of students gathered last week. Robin pulled a manila envelope out of the canvas bag slung over her shoulder. She'd printed out color copies of Green Girl, Niesha, the maker's mark, and the man with the dragonfly tattoo.

"See any dragonfly shirts?" Robin asked, shading her eyes against the July glare.

"No, but..." Amy discreetly pointed to a group sitting on the steps in front of one of the residence halls. "Let's go talk to them."

"Okay, Teach. You're the brave one. You lead."

Wanting to appear as gutsy as her cousin apparently thought she was, Amy squared her shoulders and held out her hand. "Give me Niesha's picture." With more bravado than she actually felt, she approached the three young women and two men who didn't look old enough to be in college. Had late teens and twentysomethings looked this young when she'd attended CSC?

"Hi!" One of the young men waved before she had a chance to interrupt their conversation. "Can we help you?"

Impressively polite. "We hope so." Amy held out the photograph. "Do any of you know her?"

The one who had greeted her looked at the brunette seated next to him. It appeared he was waiting for a green light from her to answer the question. When she gave a slight nod, without looking at Amy, he said, "We all do. She's in our Bible study."

Seeing the fish symbol on the jar had made Amy wonder if Niesha was a Christian. Amy's heart warmed at the confirmation. "We've heard she left school. Do any of you know where she went?"

Again, the coded glances followed by an almost imperceptible nod. "Are you cops?" the young man asked.

"No. We're just concerned about her."

Raking his fingers through short blond hair, he said, "We are too. We told campus police last week we thought her boyfriend might have done something to her, but then he was here two days ago, looking for her."

Amy glanced at Robin then the envelope. Robin slid out the picture of the man with the tattoo.

He scowled. "That's him. Emmett."

Emmett. Finally, something to go on. "Do you know his last name, or anything about him?"

A young woman with long black hair and porcelain skin shook her head. "I only saw them together once. Never met him until he came around asking if we knew where she was. He told us not to tell anyone he was here."

Robin pulled a business card from her purse and handed it to her. "If you hear anything or think of anything else, would you mind letting us know? After you inform the police, of course. We're praying for Niesha."

The woman took the card. Robin and Amy thanked them and started to walk away.

"Wait!" The brunette stood up. "Her boyfriend was wearing a security guard uniform."

"Campus security?" Robin asked.

"No. It was a gray uniform with SECURITY in red on the back. He had a patch on his shoulder. Shaped like a stop sign." She turned to the young man she'd been sending wordless messages to. "Did you see a company name?"

He shook his head. "Wish I had."

"Thank you," Amy said. "You should probably report that. Seemingly insignificant details can make or break an investigation." It was a line she'd recently heard on a CSI show.

As they headed toward the Herrick Center, Matt suddenly yelled, "Hey! There's Pastor Gary! What's he doing here?" He waved wildly, ran to the gray-haired man, and flung his arms around his waist.

Amy smiled, her heart swelling with pride and gratitude. So many godly men had stepped up in the past two months to fill the father hole in Matt's heart.

After they exchanged greetings, Pastor Gary explained that he led a weekly Bible study on campus. The cousins locked gazes. Without needing an exchange of words, Robin pulled out the photos and showed him Niesha's picture.

His countenance seemed to darken. He sighed. "Niesha. How do you two know her?"

"We don't, actually," Amy answered. "What can you tell us about her?"

Smile lines bracketed his mouth. "She's a brand-new believer. She gave her heart to the Lord about two months ago." His smile faded. "She didn't show up at last week's study, and I just heard a couple of days ago that she's left school. No one I've talked to seems to know anything."

"We heard the same thing." Robin showed him the picture of the guy with the dragonfly tattoo. "This is her boyfriend. Emmett something. Do you know him?"

"I never met him, but she talked about him. She said he was asking what she called 'God questions.'" He made air quotes around the two words.

"Do you know anything about Niesha's family?" Robin asked. "Did she grow up around here?"

"This is public record, so I think it's all right to tell you." He glanced at Matt. "Niesha was in the foster care system. She spent her high school years in a group home in St. Louis. I don't know much about her life before that." He shook his head. "I'm guessing you have reason to believe she's in trouble."

Amy did her best to give him the abridged version of the reason for their quest, starting with finding the painting at the flea market.

Pastor Gary listened intently then slowly nodded. "That painting was stolen a couple of years before I came to Faith Chapel, but I distinctly remember two conversations about it. The first was with a friend of Pearl's who called me from Michigan."

"Elizabeth Blair?"

"Ah. Yes. I'd only been pastoring here a few weeks when she called and said she was very worried that Pearl, who'd only been widowed a few years, was getting involved with the…" He stopped, then smiled sheepishly. "Probably shouldn't be discussing that."

"We know you can't repeat confidences," Amy said, "but if there's anything you could tell us that would help us unravel this mystery, we'd be grateful."

He set his briefcase on the sidewalk. "There is one thing. Probably not a confidence I need to keep now that she's gone, and I can't imagine it will be of any help to you anyway. I asked her, years ago, if they ever found the person who stole her painting, and she gave me a cryptic answer I never did decipher. She said, 'Pastor, do you think Corrie ten Boom's family was wrong to hide those Jewish people from the Nazis?'"

Chapter Eight

Pastor Gary shrugged. "We had a lively discussion about ethics after that, but she never actually answered my question. Any idea what she meant?"

Amy looked at Robin, who appeared as confused as Amy felt. "No idea," Amy answered. *The Hiding Place*, the story of Corrie ten Boom's Dutch Christian family who sheltered Jews during World War II then ended up in a concentration camp, had been on Grandma Pearl's "required" summer reading list. Robin and Amy had both read it. "Do you think she was asking if it's all right to lie if you're protecting someone?" She explained their thought that Grandma might have been "doing the Romans 12 thing."

"I can easily imagine her doing that," he said. His gaze drifted across the campus. "I'm sorry. I seem to have only stirred up more questions."

"That's all we're running into lately," Robin said. "The answer to one question brings up two more. We found a newspaper clipping of the theft of the painting. It said Elizabeth Blair was the one who reported it missing. That seemed odd."

Pastor Gary pressed his lips together. "Maybe your grandmother was too much in shock. Was the painting sentimental? Passed down in her family or given as a gift?"

"She told us she knew the woman in the painting, but that's all we know. She seemed to enjoy giving those cryptic answers. Anytime we asked her about it, she answered with a question."

"Very mysterious. Have you talked to anyone else as...seasoned... as I am who would remember back that far?"

"My mom and Columbia Burke. They both confirmed what you've said. Grandma Pearl thought people were making too big a deal out of one missing painting."

"Strange," he said. "Where has it been all these years? How in the world did Niesha Carter end up with a painting stolen from Pearl Allen's house thirty-plus years ago?"

"That's exactly what we're trying to figure out." Amy glanced at her watch. "We need to get going. We have an appointment to talk to an art history professor. We'll get in touch with you if we hear anything."

"I'll do the same." He glanced heavenward. "Lord, Niesha is in Your hands. Please keep her safe."

"Amen." Matt's voice rose above Amy's and Robin's, and Pastor Gary laid a hand on his head. Amy knew he was offering up a prayer of blessing for her son.

The little woman, who might not reach the five-foot mark, wore giant, black-framed glasses on a face with enough creases and lines to make Jeff's assessment of her age understandable. She not only taught history, she'd lived it. Amy guessed she was at least eighty. Evidently, the word *retirement* was not in her vocabulary.

Maura Childs ushered them in and motioned to four leather chairs arranged in front of a gleaming oak desk. In sharp contrast to Professor Douglas's cluttered domain, only a phone, a pair of sunglasses, a pencil holder, a yellow legal pad, and an open hardcover book sat on the polished expanse. After introductions, in which she asked them to call her Maura, the professor extended her hand to Matt. "Is the college in your future, young man?"

"Probably. Uncle Jeff says it's the best school in Missouri."

She gave a surprisingly hearty laugh for a woman her size. "He is absolutely right." Turning to Amy she said, "You're Jeff's sister-in-law."

"Yes." She hadn't planned on bringing that up. They weren't sure what the professor would think about the nosy women with a child in tow, sleuthing around campus like amateur private investigators. "He speaks highly of you," Amy said. She tried not to smile when she remembered Jeff's actual comments.

"Jeff mentioned you've been looking for Niesha Carter. I know who she is but haven't had her in class yet. I've heard the buzz among the faculty. No one seems to know anything. Have you learned her whereabouts?"

"Not yet." Robin set the large envelope on her lap. "We've talked to several students who know her. They said her boyfriend was on campus a couple of days ago asking about her."

"One of our faculty members speculated that she may have run off with a love interest. Apparently, that's not the case." She shook her head. After a moment her face brightened. "Jeff sounded all kinds of mysterious about why you wanted to talk to me."

"He thought you might be able to give us some insight into a painting that belonged to our grandmother." Robin dug in the envelope and handed her the photograph of Green Girl.

Amy was sure the hazel eyes magnified by thick lenses widened when Maura looked at the image. She blinked and seemed to be trying to hide her initial surprise, but the lines on her wizened face deepened as she studied it. Her free hand toyed with the pearl button of her high-necked white blouse. "Wh-what were you hoping to find out about it?"

"There isn't a signature, so we're wondering if you know who the artist is or when it was painted."

"Of course, I can't tell much from a photograph." She opened a drawer and pulled out a small magnifying glass. After studying the picture for a moment—a moment in which Amy was sure a muscle at the corner of Maura's eye began to twitch—she said, "Tell me what you know about this. It belonged to your grandmother? When did you see it last?"

An odd question. One cardinal rule Amy had learned by watching crime scene investigation shows was not to show your hand too soon. Let the suspect walk into the trap all on his or, in this case, *her* own. They hadn't mentioned that the painting was stolen. Had Jeff told her? Not that she was a likely suspect, but she was acting strange. It would be beyond coincidence if they'd just happened to stumble upon the culprit, but she was around in 1987. "We saw it this week," she said. "It belongs to the family."

Maura's penciled-on eyebrows started to rise, but she quickly reined in her surprise. Again. "When did your grandmother purchase it?"

"We don't know. It was hanging in her house when we were kids," Robin answered.

Very smooth, Rob. Amy would remember to commend her. "Does it look like the work of a local artist?" she asked the professor. "Anyone you're familiar with?"

Maura closed one eye and squinted. "Hard to tell from this. If I could see it in person, the textures and brushstrokes might tell me something. So it's been in your family for decades at least?"

Robin nodded.

"Was it framed that whole time?"

Another odd question. "For many years," Amy said. "We've recently started looking for a new frame."

Maura wound a stray silvering curl around a bony finger. "Was there anything identifying on the back of the canvas? Anything written on it that could help us…you trace it to an original owner maybe?"

This time she would not give anything more away. "No name," Amy answered evasively. "Nothing that would tell us anything about the artist."

"What about the painting in the background?" Robin asked. "Can you tell us anything about it? Does it look like it was painted by the same artist?"

Still holding the photograph, the professor opened the middle drawer of her desk and returned the magnifying glass. As she closed the drawer, the cover of the book on the desk snapped closed. With what appeared to be forced casualness, she deftly opened it again. But not before Amy read the title on the spine.

Maura ran a fingertip across her upper lip. "Hard to be certain. I will do some research for you." She tapped the photo. "May I keep this?" She slid her chair back and stood.

Evidently, their meeting was over.

Matt burst through the main door ahead of Amy and Robin and walked backward, or rather, skipped backward, in front of them. "She knows something! I actually heard her swallow. And did you see how she played with that button and wiped her face? She's old. She could have stolen the painting thirty-five years ago, right? Maybe somebody stole it from her after she stole it from Grandma Pearl." His eyes bugged. "Now she knows we have it. That's why she kept saying she wanted to look at it for real and not just in the picture. But she doesn't know *where* we have it. Yet. Uncle Jeff better get security cameras and a smart deadbolt lock he can program from his phone. And we need to tell the police to drive by their house at random times of the day and watch for—"

"Stop!" Half laughing and half wondering how often Matt hid on the stairs watching her TV shows after his bedtime, Amy held up a traffic cop hand. "I'm pretty sure Professor Maura Childs is not going to break in and steal Green Girl. Not single-handedly anyway."

Robin swooped in and grabbed Matt's cheeks in both of her hands. She was far more than half laughing. "How does all that fit in a ten-year-old brain?" She let him go, and Amy basked in the glow of his smile.

"Well, somebody has to watch out for this family!" He grinned and spun on his heel, leading the way to the parking lot.

Please God, please God...

Robin's arm slid around her waist. As if reading her mind, she said, "God's got this. All of it."

"I know. At least in my head I do. My heart lags behind sometimes."

"I get that." Robin tightened her hug, then dropped her arm. "So do you think boy genius is right?"

Amy thought about the diminutive professor's behavior. "Something was definitely weird. Matt's right, she was fidgeting and swallowing hard. We need to find out what Jeff...the book!" Amy stopped walking and clamped her eyes shut. "I saw the title of the book she was reading and then she deliberately covered it up. I caught the first few words and the last one. Nazis."

Robin's eyes widened. "You really think she wanted to hide it?"

"Definitely. She was trying to do it nonchalantly, but I'm sure it was deliberate. She didn't want us to see it." Amy attempted to make the first words form in her brain. "It was Greek. The 'Something-Greek-starting-with-an-O Clock.' I know I've heard the Greek name. Like a hundred years ago in a mythology class. Odessa? Or Olympia?" She opened her eyes and handed her car keys to Robin. "You drive, I'll search."

When they got to the car and she told Matt why Robin was driving, Matt gave a fist pump. "Cool. Another clue."

As Robin drove back to the store, Amy typed *Greek Mythological Character names starting with O* into the search engine on her phone. A list popped up. "Ocalea, Oceanus, Odysseus, Olympus,

Onchestus, Oreads, Orpheus. That's it! *The Orpheus Clock.*" She keyed in the name, ready to read the book's description. But the subtitle froze her. "Guys…listen to this: *The Orpheus Clock: The Search for My Family's Art Treasures Stolen by the Nazis.*"

Robin shot her a look then pulled to the side of the road.

"Whoa." Matt unclicked his seat belt and scooted forward in the back seat. "Pastor Gary said Grandma Pearl was talking about the Nazis."

Robin gave a slow nod. "And…*stolen* art treasures?"

Amy knew she mirrored her cousin's stunned expression. "And Arthur Douglas had a report about Nazi art plunder on his desk." She hugged her arms. "What are we getting ourselves into?"

September 26, 1937

Well, today did not turn out even close to how I imagined it would all week. It was such a beautiful, clear-sky day and just the perfect temperature for a picnic. After church, the men assembled tables out of boards and sawhorses and the women draped them with tablecloths. I thought the food table would break in half with all the covered dishes! Barbeque and fried chicken and corn bread and baked beans. The boys all took turns cranking the ice cream freezers while we older girls set out the toppings. There were jars of peaches and cherries and apple pie filling. Mom brought her scrumptious strawberry rhubarb sauce, and Mrs. Martin brought two jars of her creamy fudge sauce. It all looked so delicious, but I couldn't make myself eat more than a couple of bites because all I could think about was the pie auction and who would bid on mine. I was scared no one would, and then I was scared the wrong person would. All week I pictured sitting with John while he looked dreamy-eyed at my cream pie and said it was the best he'd ever eaten.

That's not what happened. John did bid on my pie. And won. But he also bid on Bess's rhubarb pie. I confess I was mad and very confused. He doesn't even like rhubarb! I figured he was just being nice, but once we sat down, I found out what he was doing. He ate a slice of each pie and said they were delicious, and then he pulled out a letter he'd gotten from Germany on Friday. A letter from his girlfriend.

John has a girlfriend.

I bet I said those words a hundred times today. I don't know why it upset me so much. After all, I have a boyfriend! It's not like I was interested in him in that way or anything. At least, I don't think I was. Maybe it's just that I wanted him to be only my friend. That is very, very selfish and unkind, but if I can't be honest here in my diary, I can't be honest anywhere. We haven't had time to talk about it, but I think Bess was sad too, or angry maybe, because she did like him in that way.

Anyway, his girlfriend's name is Gänse Sommer—I had to ask him to write it for me—and her family is planning to immigrate here soon. It's clear that John is madly in love with her. He says she plays the piano and "sings like a bird" and her English is even better than his. He thinks we will like her very much, and he is probably right. I think I am already over any silly ideas I had about keeping John all to myself. It will be fun to have a new friend, and I really think he and Richard will like each other.

My English teacher wants us all to write to someone in another country. Pen pals, she calls them. Maybe I will ask for Gänse's address, and then I'll have a pen pal in Germany!

Oh! I forgot to tell you something. Since today was so much fun, some of us decided to have another party in two weeks. We are calling it the Faith Chapel Harvest Festival. Everyone must come in costume!

Good night, dear diary!

Chapter Nine

The kids were bathed and in bed by eight thirty on Thursday night. Amy stepped onto the porch with her phone, a bottle of water, and a copy of *This Old House* magazine. She'd had it for several days, waiting for just the right time to reward herself. Since she'd finished painting the half bath off the kitchen after supper, this was the perfect night to relax on the porch and dream. First, she needed to check the texts and emails she'd ignored over the last few hours. Funny how just a few months ago she never would have let this much time pass without checking messages and her social media. She thought of a card she'd recently sent a friend in Steelville who'd had her first baby. The picture on the front showed a tiny hand in a larger one and the caption read, *Motherhood changes everything*. No truer words.

She scanned emails. Nothing urgent. There were two unread text messages. Her jaw tensed when she realized one, sent around six o'clock, was from Melanie. It was unusual for the social worker to text rather than call. She held her breath as she tapped on the message.

JANELLE AND DILLON HAVE REQUESTED A VISIT WITH JANA. WOULD SUNDAY AFTERNOON AT 4:00 WORK? THEY ARE WILLING TO MEET HALFWAY, AT A PARK IN FARBER. I WILL SUPERVISE.

Amy's mouth went dry. She couldn't swallow. *Lord...please.* Jana would be with both of her biological parents for the first time in more than two years. After the kids' last visit with Janelle in May, just before they'd moved to Canton, Jana hadn't slept for two nights. When Amy asked if she'd had fun, she'd vehemently shaken her head. According to Melanie, Jana hadn't spoken the whole time. Though Amy had tried to get her to express her feelings, Jana wasn't able to put them into words. Was she afraid of her mother? Or angry at her for giving them up?

How would she explain to Matt that his mother only wanted to see Jana and not him? Amy's hand curled into a fist. She knew the reason. Dillon was not Matt's father. Janelle wouldn't want to overwhelm him with the thought of caring for two children, a task he clearly hadn't warmed to in the past. But surely, if they got back together, they would take both of them, wouldn't they? She wondered how often her new mama heart could squeeze this tight and still keep beating.

With a deep breath, she answered the text. 4:00 ON SUNDAY IN FARBER WILL WORK.

She supposed she should at least be grateful for their offer to meet halfway. When she'd accepted the responsibility of transporting Matt and Jana to parental visits, she'd assumed there wouldn't be any.

She leaned against the back of the swing and pushed on the old porch boards with bare feet, setting it in motion. Slowing her breathing, she tried to focus on the buzz of locusts and the midsummer chorus of the katydids. The sky between trees and rooflines glowed vermilion and a slight breeze rose, just enough to ruffle the red oak's pointy leaves.

Breathe. Relax. Trust. A year ago, she would have said she had a strong faith. She trusted God to direct her path. Her faith had held firm even when her parents died. She'd survived two painful boyfriend breakups, seeing each as God's intervention in relationships that weren't right for her. But none of these losses had tested her trust in the Lord like this one. Grandma Pearl had often said, "Love with open hands." Amy hadn't really understood those words until now. How did she meet the needs of children in desperate need of love and yet stay detached enough to not implode if they went back to their mother?

When she'd first looked into fostering, it was with purely altruistic motives. She'd had too many students over the years who were hungry for security and needed someone to be a stable influence. She'd seen foster parenting as a way to offer a helping hand. Assuming she would be giving temporary care, that children would pass in and out of her life, hopefully better off because of her time and attention, she hadn't been prepared for discovering it would be impossible to open her home and not her heart.

She flipped two pages in the magazine and tried to focus on kitchen ideas. With Jeff and Tracy's recommendations, she'd hired an electrician, plumber, and carpenter to get the house up to the standards needed to be licensed as a foster home in Lewis County. Though up to code, the house still needed a lot of TLC. She hadn't made as much as she'd hoped on the sale of her Steelville house, so most of her inheritance from Grandma Pearl had gone into purchasing this one. Not much remained for the kind of projects she saw on the pages of *This Old House*. By budgeting paychecks wisely, she'd tackle them one at a time. *Just like I need to handle everything in my life.* God wouldn't give her more than He would help her handle.

She stared at glossy photos of white cupboards framed by pale, spring-green walls. It would be the perfect shade to coordinate with the Depression glass Grandma had given her over the years. A tiny surge of adrenaline countered the tension in her neck. With happier thoughts dancing in her head, maybe she would sleep tonight after all.

Winking lights washed the porch as a car turned the corner. Thoughts on spring-green walls, she watched it absentmindedly. A black SUV. The streetlamp illuminated a crumpled front fender. The passenger side headlight bobbed like a blinking eyeball. Moments later, the same vehicle passed again, this time in front of her house, driving slowly, as if searching for an address. She thought she saw movement in the passenger side, but it was too dark to be sure. The driver accelerated, and the SUV barreled through the intersection and out of sight.

Amy chided herself for the unsettled feeling left in the vehicle's wake. The mood set by Melanie's text had activated her hair-trigger imagination. She would not let it take on a life of its own.

She would *not*.

Closing the magazine, she got up and walked inside, locking the door behind her.

"We're out of chicken nuggets." Matt stood in front of a freezer case at County Market on Friday morning.

Amy opened the glass door, pulled out two bags, and tossed them in her cart. "Go get a bag of fries to go with it." Tonight would be easy. She hoped to spend a couple of hours sorting pictures in Grandma's attic, and it would be nice not to have to think about cooking when she got home. She smiled down at Jana, who'd been walking through most of the store hugging a box of Fruity Pebbles. Once a month, she allowed them to pick a "fun" cereal, and Jana wasn't letting this one out of her sight. Amy smiled at her. "Can you pick out a veggie for supper?"

"*Any* vegetable?"

Amy smiled at the look of wonder in Jana's eyes. "Yep. Your choice." Back in November she'd been astonished to discover how many things she thought of as being part of every child's reality that Matt and Jana had never experienced. Thanksgiving dinner, Christmas stockings, sledding, water balloons, s'mores, fresh fruit they could help themselves to without asking. From what she could gather, their diet before moving in with her had consisted mostly of canned beans, bologna, white bread, and Oreos. Six months ago, they'd both had the dull hair and translucent skin associated with malnutrition, but no one could guess that now. At first, she'd banished sugar and anything processed, but since they'd moved to Canton, she'd started adding what she thought of as memory-maker foods. Every week they made pizza on Fridays, sundaes on Sunday, and roasted marshmallows in the firepit out in the backyard.

The familiar sound of squabbling drew Amy's attention to a tug of war over a bag of vegetables. With a sigh, she walked to Matt and Jana and held out her hand. Matt set the bag in her palm with a bit more force than needed.

"She knows I hate broccoli," he whined.

Since when? Amy didn't voice the thought.

Jana made a face at her brother. "You called it trees and cheese and said you loved it."

"That was before. Now I only like corn."

"Whoa. Stop." Amy rested a hand on Matt's shoulder. *Pick your battles.* It was one of the best bits of parenting advice she'd ever received. "We have corn at home. I asked Jana to pick out a vegetable for tonight, and she made a good choice."

"I agree." The woman's voice came from behind Amy. She swiveled to see Grace Park, Canton's head librarian, selecting a frozen dinner.

"Hi, Grace. How are you?"

"Couldn't be better." She put a boxed meal in her cart and stepped to the side. "I was actually going to give Tracy a call after I got to the library today. I don't know that it will help you with your mystery, but I did a search for Pearl in our files of Columbia Burke's Cantonbury Tales column. I found one from May 13, 1987, a week after the painting was reported stolen."

Amy held up one finger to Matt, who was clearly anxious to say something, most likely about broccoli, and turned her full attention on Grace. "What did it say?"

Grace pulled out her phone. "Here."

Under the Cantonbury Tales heading was a subtitle: CHANGES TO CANTON TOUR OF HOMES.

Sadly, the fourth annual Canton Tour of Homes, a fundraiser for the Canton Historical Society, is losing one of its most prestigious stops this year. The stately Allen home has been withdrawn from the roster. Mrs. Pearl Allen was unavailable for comment. I'm sure all of you join me in hoping we will see her magnificent specimen of Midwestern Victorian architecture in our lineup next season and that this year's fundraising success will not be hindered by its absence.

"Hmm." Amy scanned the article again, not liking the feelings it evoked. "We met with Columbia. She mentioned calling Grandma Pearl right after the theft and said Grandma was upset with her and she didn't know why. Seems pretty obvious to me. This is nothing short of a blatant guilt trip."

"That's what I thought," Grace agreed. "I know Columbia had a reputation for being blunt, but this seems just plain manipulative. Though they were pretty close friends. Is it possible to read this in a humorous tone?"

Amy tried. "I suppose Columbia could have meant it as gentle chiding and Grandma misinterpreted it."

Grace smiled. "I guess it was as easy to read our own interpretation into the written word back then as we do with texting now."

"True. Thank you for finding this. We need all the help we can get."

"This is exciting. The life of a librarian is not laden with an overabundance of intrigue." Grace winked. "Well, I better get going. I'll let you know if I find anything else."

Questions swirled in Amy's mind as she turned back to her charges. Matt bounced on his heels. While wiggling both eyebrows, he pointed behind his hand. "Over there," he whispered.

Amy stared at the endcap display of ice cream toppings for a moment before it registered that Matt wasn't directing her attention to the hot fudge, but to the young woman looking at it. A young brunette with a long braid, wearing a pale blue T-shirt with a dragonfly logo on the front.

With a barely perceptible nod, Amy whispered, "Stay close to Jana," and, as casually as she could, walked slowly toward the woman who held a jar of caramel sauce in her hand. "Have you tried that brand?" she asked.

"Huh? Oh. Yeah. It's the best." Her voice was flat. She seemed distracted, as if her mind was somewhere else.

"I noticed your shirt. Do you know Niesha Carter?"

The young woman looked straight at her. Amy had the feeling she was being studied. "How do you know her?"

"I really like her work." She was tempted to imply she knew Niesha personally, but quickly talked herself out of anything smacking of deception. Though maybe there was nothing unethical about a little name dropping. "I talked to Pastor Gary Bennett, who leads a Bible study Niesha was in. I was sad to hear she'd left school." Amy steadied her voice, forcing calm into her demeanor. "Do you have contact with her?"

With a glance at Amy's cart and then at Matt and Jana, as if trying to decide whether she was a person to be trusted, she nodded. "Kind of."

Amy's pulse tripped. "Do you know Emmett?"

The young woman nodded again then looked around as if afraid he'd be listening.

"I know some of her friends think she may be in danger, possibly from him." Amy kept her tone steady. "Is that true?"

"Maybe. I don't know where she is." Her eyes reddened. "I got a message from her asking me to check for messages from her every day in case she needed to reach me. I thought maybe Emmett had taken her, like kidnapped her, but I heard he was looking for her on campus. I think she's hiding from him."

The confirmation of Amy's concerns brought a wave of sadness tinged with fear. "What's Emmett's last name?"

"I don't know. Sounds dumb, right? But she was always very secretive about him." She wiped her eyes with the back of her hand. "I don't know what he was into, but it might not have been legal. Niesha thought he was changing. She said he had a lot of questions about God, and he was really listening to everything she told him. But I think she was just hearing what she wanted to hear. She has a big heart like that, always seeing the best in people even when she shouldn't. I think he was playing her, pretending to go along with what she was interested in. Maybe he was trying to get her to work for him. I don't know. She found something that scared her. She wouldn't tell me what it was. Drugs, maybe. I think that's why she's running. He knows she figured out what he's up to, and he's going to silence her."

Amy tried to calm her racing pulse. Maybe much of this was theatrics. "Have you talked to the police?"

The dark braid bobbed against one shoulder. "I told them she was missing, and that I thought Emmett was involved. I showed them his picture. But I don't know where he lives, and Niesha got rid of her phone because she was afraid of being tracked, so I don't know…how…" She looked at Amy with pleading eyes.

"You said she messaged you, but she doesn't have a phone. Was she sending messages through social media? From a laptop or other device?" Amy forced herself to stop at two questions.

"We have a…secret way."

It was clear she didn't want to be pressed for details.

Amy bit her bottom lip. *Lord, I need wisdom here.* "I would love to help her if possible. Can I stay in contact with you?"

Again, the furtive glances. "I…don't know. I don't know you."

"Understood. I'm Amy Allen. How about if I give you my number in case you learn something?" The look of fear on the girl's face twisted Amy's heart. "Do you know Pastor Gary?"

She nodded. "I'm in his Bible study."

"Why don't you call him and ask him about me. My sister and cousin and I are worried about Niesha. He's helping us look for her."

Following another moment of hesitation, the young woman pulled out her phone, unlocked it, and handed it to Amy. "If you know Pastor Gary, I think I can trust you. I'm Lisa."

"Nice to meet you, Lisa." Amy typed Lisa's name into a text to herself. That way, she'd also have Lisa's number. "Please call anytime, even if you just want to talk. I'll be praying for Niesha."

Lisa wiped a tear rolling down her cheek and walked away. Without the caramel sauce.

Chapter Ten

*A*my sat cross-legged on the floor in what she'd come to call her "picture corner" in Grandma's attic. Matt was at a birthday party for his friend Blake, and Jana was playing quietly with the wooden dolls. Tracy would be home for lunch any minute.

A few moments of quiet. Amy breathed in the musty smell that brought her back to her childhood. So many Saturday afternoons sitting up here with Grandma Pearl, listening to tales of "the olden days." She'd talked about the German customs handed down for generations. Grandma was in the fourth generation on her father's side born in the US. Her father had fought in World War I. Against the Germans. What about after that? Was there anything connecting her family to the Nazis? Anything that would explain Grandma's question about hiding Jews?

German prisoners of war had been held in hundreds of camps in the United States. Were there any in Missouri? She pulled out her phone and was shocked to see the numbers. Four hundred and twenty thousand German and Italian prisoners of war had spent part of World War II under guard in the United States. Fifteen thousand of them were housed in Missouri. Another article grabbed her attention. The heading read: JUNE 16, 1945 THE DAY GERMAN POWs ESCAPED THEIR CAMP NEAR ST. LOUIS.

Nazi soldiers, fleeing from a camp a hundred and twenty-some miles from Canton. Could there possibly be some connection to Grandma Pearl? Or her parents? They were German. Could they have given shelter to a POW? She didn't want to think that was possible.

Amy had given a speech in college about what the world knew and when about the horrors inflicted by Hitler's minions. She'd memorized part of a 1941 radio broadcast by Churchill. Bits and pieces floated into her mind. *As Hitler's armies advance, whole districts are being exterminated. Scores of thousands…executions in cold blood…perpetrated by the German police troops.… And this is but the beginning. Famine and pestilence have yet to follow in the bloody ruts of Hitler's tanks.* She remembered the last line as if she'd memorized it yesterday. *We are in the presence of a crime without a name.*

She massaged her right temple as she continued to read about the prisoners. Only two men escaped. They left a note saying they could not return to Germany, because it would only be exchanging life under a Nazi dictatorship for living under Russian tyranny. Wouldn't her great-grandparents have been sympathetic to their plight? She breathed out a sigh as she scanned the next paragraph. The men had only made it ten miles before being captured.

"Find anything?"

Amy startled at Tracy's interruption. She shook her head. "Just an interesting rabbit trail. Get that article done?"

"Yes. Not my best. The 1929 flood is interesting, but I didn't find anything new. I need something fresh." Tracy sat on a stool and took a bite out of a sandwich. "You know, I used to come home and relax on my lunch break."

Amy laughed and handed her phone to Tracy. "Ever write about the POW camp in Chesterfield during World War II?"

"No." Tracy scanned the page. "Are you thinking this has something to do with Grandma's question about the Nazis?"

"That's what led me there, but no. I'm back to square one." She swept her arm out. "All of this family history. There has to be something here that will get us on the right track."

"We haven't touched any of this yet." Tracy walked to the window where two rows of wood crates, trunks, and cardboard boxes lined the wall beneath the windowsill. Some were marked with labels like *Grandma Allen's Knickknacks, Salt and Pepper Shakers*, and several labeled in Grandma's hand: *Howard—sort these!*

Amy set aside the box she'd been looking through before wandering off on her dead-end goose chase. "Maybe we should tackle a couple of the unlabeled boxes."

"I'm game. I'll start on this end if you want to start over there." Tracy pointed to the right side of the wall.

They worked in silence for several minutes. Tracy sat on a wooden crate with a box of letters on her lap. "These are all from the forties and fifties," she said.

"Might find a clue in there," Amy answered, sliding her fingers under loose tape on a warped cardboard box. It was her third one. The first two had contained clothes from what appeared to be the 1970s.

The box was filled with newspaper-wrapped bundles. She uncovered a music box with a twirling ballerina wrapped in newsprint from 1963. Next, she found a gold-framed hand mirror and a book of prayers with a copyright date of 1934. A flat package lay on the bottom. Lightweight, about a foot square. She freed it from its paper shroud. An unframed canvas with a painting of a castle with mountains in the background. A familiar castle. She turned it over and read the writing on the back. *Neuschwanstein 1935.*

"Look." She held it up for Tracy. "It says 1935 on the back."

Tracy took it and held it close to the window. "These brushstrokes...," she whispered.

Amy stepped closer. As Tracy tipped the canvas toward the light, the raised strokes became clear. Short, distinct brush marks. She looked up, locking eyes with her sister. "Do you think—"

"Sure could be."

"What in the world are you two up to?"

Startled by the unexpected voice, Amy teetered on the chair she was standing on in front of the family room fireplace. She stared at Robin. "What are *you* up to?"

Tracy jumped down from the chair she was standing on. "I told her we might have found something."

"She told me to come over after work," Robin said. "So, as the boss, I declared a half day. Show me what you found." She stepped onto the chair Tracy had vacated.

"We discovered this in the attic." Amy pointed at the castle painting leaning on the mantel. Tracy handed Robin the magnifying glass she'd been using.

Without a word, Robin studied the castle, then zoomed close to Green Girl, then held the castle up next to the larger painting. She let out a low whistle and turned the small canvas over. "*Neuschwanstein*, 1935. You're thinking this was painted by the same artist?"

Tracy and Amy nodded in unison.

"So, if Green Girl was painted during the lifetime of an artist who worked in 1935, and we take an educated guess that he or she had to have been between twenty and eighty in 1935, we could be looking at any time from the 1880s to…what's the earliest date we know it was hanging here?"

"Mom was born in 1946," Robin said. "We've got family pictures when she was a baby with Green Girl in the background. Who knows how long it was there before that."

Amy rubbed both temples. "Between the 1880s and 1940s is a pretty big window, but at least we know it's not ancient."

"Disney!" Jana shouted. Amy had told her to bring the wooden dolls down to the living room, and she'd been too busy setting them up on the coffee table to pay attention to the adults. She pointed at the smaller painting. "That's the princess castle."

"Almost," Amy said. "This is a castle way over in Germany that the Disney people used as a model for the princess castle."

"It's pretty," Jana said, then went back to positioning the dolls on miniature wooden chairs.

"I made cookies this morning," Tracy said. "Sugar might help us think." She motioned for them to follow her into the kitchen. Amy and Robin sat at the table while Tracy poured glasses of tea and arranged chocolate chip cookies on a plate.

"I almost forgot." Robin held up her phone. "I found something. I did a search for security companies. The patch Emmett was wearing is from Overland Protective Services. It looks like a pretty small new start-up based in Quincy."

Amy took a sip of the sweet tea Tracy set in front of her. "I don't suppose we'd find out anything by giving them a call."

Robin tipped her head to one side. "How do we explain wanting information about a guy we've never met and don't know anything about?"

Tracy joined them at the table. "At least we have his first name now, so we don't have to walk in asking for information about a big bald guy with a dragonfly tattoo. We'll probably still look like crazy ladies though."

"Maybe that's okay." Amy picked up a cookie and broke it in half. The chocolate was still gooey. "Maybe we should just be our quirky selves. Personally, I think we're endearing." She wrinkled her nose at her sister and cousin before sinking her teeth into the soft, chewy cookie.

"I nominate you again." Robin used a cookie to point at Amy. "Call them and be crazy endearing."

Amy shook her head. "We need to go there. If we call, we might not get beyond a receptionist. They need to see our adorable faces." She waved her fingertips toward her face. "I mean, who could say no to this?" She batted her eyes. After weeks of feeling she was walking under a cloud, it felt good to be silly.

"Well…I happen to have the rest of the day off." Robin wiggled her eyebrows at Tracy. "Can't you call this research for a story? I mean, once we solve this, you will write about it."

"I guess I probably will." Tracy pursed her lips. "Okay. I'm in. Can you get a sitter on short notice, Amy?"

Hand sliding over her phone, Amy nodded. "I'm sure I can."

"Supper at Dunnbelly?" Tracy suggested.

Amy grinned. "I can definitely get a sitter!" The bistro, about half an hour south and across the river, specialized in "comfort food classics," and was one of her favorites. "Best Baja shrimp tacos anywhere."

Robin gave a thumbs-up. "Do you think we should show the castle painting to Professor Douglas just to see his reaction?"

"Maybe," Amy answered. "I wish we could find out something about it first. Did Grandma know the artist or did she just like his work?"

"And what's the connection with Germany? In 1935, Grandma would have been…thirteen? Did she and her family go to Germany?"

Amy, who'd been an avid fan of World War II novels and documentaries since college, said, "Things were starting to become unstable by then. Hitler was defying the League of Nations and broke the Treaty of Versailles by commissioning submarines. Not a great time to visit, though it's possible."

"There are other paintings in the attic," Tracy said. "I think we should look at them. After our little field trip."

Amy sent Olivia a text about babysitting the kids and got an immediate "Love to!" in response. Something niggled in the back of her mind. She had the same feeling she got when hovering over a jigsaw puzzle, holding a piece and searching for its rightful place. If she could just find where it fit, a portion of the picture would finally come clear.

The castle. What was it about the castle that seemed to be a link that would pull together some of their unconnected clues?

"I need to check something." She entered *Neuschwanstein Castle Nazis* into her phone.

At the top of the list that resulted was an article titled "Neuschwanstein: A Fairy Tale Setting's Dark Nazi Past."

"Trace, Rob, listen to this." She began to read, "'George Clooney's World War II drama, *The Monuments Men*, follows an Allied special forces unit tasked with uncovering and protecting Europe's stolen treasures during the Second World War. One of the major depots for hiding stolen art is a location we now associate with Disney World and fairy tales.

"'Eccentric King Ludwig II did not construct the whimsical Neuschwanstein Castle for royal purposes. He designed it as a hideaway from the public. Half a century later, because of its secret tunnels, passageways, and location near the Austrian border, the castle was declared the ideal location for the headquarters of *Einsatzstab Reichsleiter Rosenberg*, the German art-looting organization.'"

Amy looked up and met wide-eyed, stunned expressions. Robin rubbed her forehead. "Wow."

"We could have stolen Nazi treasure?" Tracy's voice was barely above a whisper.

Another puzzle piece beyond their grasp. "Grandma got paid for Green Girl in 1937. If the castle was painted two years earlier..." She shook her head.

She couldn't make the pieces fit.

Tracy was right. *The more we learn, the more we don't know.*

Chapter Eleven

Driving south to La Grange on old Highway 61 added a few minutes to their trip to Quincy, but the scenic views were worth it. Robin drove, Tracy sat in the passenger seat, and Amy had the back seat to herself as they meandered along the river valley with the flat farmland bordering the Mississippi on both sides of the highway. Heat shimmered off the asphalt. The tips of cornstalks curled like outstretched tongues pleading for water.

"Looks like we're finally going to get some significant rain this weekend," Tracy said, looking at her weather app.

"Better get my buckets ready." Amy did a quick calculation in her head of how many paychecks she'd need before she could afford a whole new roof. She'd had a few spots repaired, but there was still a leak in the corner of her bedroom. Rain represented the delicate balance she saw in so many areas of her life right now. If it were up to her, she'd have the rain hold off until the end of October when she had a new roof. But the farmers desperately needed moisture in the soil. If it were up to her, she would gladly put up with rain buckets if she could call down a deluge on Sunday to cancel Janelle and Dillon's visitation plans. But how could she deny a mother the chance to see her child? No matter what poor choices Janelle had made, Amy was sure she must still love her children. Was that created-in-the-womb love more vital to Matt and Jana than what Amy could give them?

They crossed the old metal bridge spanning the Wyaconda River. A railroad bridge, rusty brown in the sunlight, ran parallel to this one. Amy commented on the low level of the murky brown water that crawled beneath the bridges. "I think I'll take the kids tubing in Steelville next week. Unless we get a ton of rain, the river should be running slow." She needed something positive to focus on.

"Sounds fun," Robin said. "Is Jana brave enough for that?"

"It's not much different from the lazy river at Splash Station, and she loved that." Unexpectedly, her voice quivered on the last few words.

Tracy turned in her seat. "You okay? You seem a little down today."

She hadn't yet told them about the visitation. Amy chided herself for sticking her head in the sand. Not talking about it wasn't going to make it go away. "I have to take Jana to meet her bio parents on Sunday."

Robin stared at her in the rearview mirror. "Oh…" So much emotion in that one word. Tracy reached over the back of the seat and grasped Amy's hand.

"So…what are we going to ask about Emmett?" Amy forced brightness into her tone as she changed the subject. She was not going to be the rain cloud on an otherwise beautiful sunny day.

Tracy squeezed her hand then let it go. "We want to know where he is and if they have any reason to suspect he may have been involved in illegal activity."

"We should ask if he had social contact with his coworkers and if any of them know Niesha," Robin added.

Amy folded her hands on her lap and leaned forward. "I wish we had a clearer hypothesis here. The painting was stolen in 1987 and appeared at a flea market two and half hours away thirty-five years later. Where was it all this time? How did Niesha end up with it? Did Emmett have anything to do with her having it? Let's come up with some guesses."

"If nothing else, it'll be fun," Tracy said.

Amy opened her notes app. "What could be a motive for someone stealing it in the first place?"

Tracy held up one finger. "Money. The thief intended to sell it." A second finger popped up. "Or just plain meanness. Which makes Elizabeth a prime suspect in my book."

Robin slowed as they neared La Grange and Highway 61 became Main Street. Now they could see the river on their left. "Since nothing else was reported stolen, it begs the question, why that specific piece of art? Grandma and Grandpa had other things of more value. Why not the cloisonné vase they got from that missionary to Japan? Or the Thomas Hart Benton painting we donated to the museum? I'm almost afraid to say out loud what that would be worth. Green Girl isn't even signed. Why did someone want that particular painting?"

"I agree with you about Elizabeth being a prime suspect. It does seem like she and Grandma had some kind of ongoing conflict," Amy said.

Robin accelerated as they passed the Mark Twain Casino, leaving La Grange behind. "Or... What if we're focusing on the wrong side of the canvas? What if this is all about the map?"

"There isn't much to it." Amy brought up the picture of the map on her phone. "Nothing labeled. Just the three lots that are starred. I mean, that's sure not nothing, but..."

Tracy nodded. "We have to figure out what, if anything, connects our house to the two others."

"Or...," Robin said again, "what if there's a secret message in the painting? Michelangelo supposedly put a bunch of hidden images on the Sistine Chapel. The flowing cloak behind God and His angels is the exact shape of the human brain. You can even pick out the vertebral artery and the pituitary gland."

"Seriously? As your son would say, that's gross." Amy laughed, and it felt good. "So what could be in Green Girl? It's kind of odd that she wasn't facing the artist and we only see her profile."

"Maybe there's a clue in the painting of the girl holding the daisy bouquet, since that seems to be what she's focused on," Tracy suggested.

Amy searched her memory for things she'd learned in a continuing education class on the Holocaust. "Did people in Europe ever use art to send messages for Jews wanting to escape? Like the legends of maps embroidered into quilts for runaway slaves to follow on the underground railroad?"

Robin nodded. "We need to research that. I've seen art that was created in concentration camps, and by people hiding from the Nazis. There's a haunting painting of a beautiful yellow butterfly perched on barbed wire, supposedly done by two artists hiding in a ghetto in Southern France. One ended up escaping like the butterfly and the other was killed at Auschwitz. Was the painting a message or just a depiction of their reality?"

They rode in silence until they reached the Mississippi and crossed under the blue-painted trusses. Old redbrick buildings and a WELCOME TO ILLINOIS—THE LAND OF LINCOLN sign greeted them. Robin turned left, and they found the building with the stop sign logo near Hampshire and Fifth.

"Ready, Amy?" Robin asked as she parallel parked.

No. She wasn't ready. She hadn't even thought about how she was going to play this out. How could she explain their interest in Emmett when she didn't even know his last name? And how could she steer the conversation around to finding out if they knew anything about Niesha's whereabouts? She thought of Lisa's conviction that Emmett was involved in something illegal. What if that was true, and he wasn't acting alone? "Did you do any research on the company, Rob? Do they have good reviews? What if it's just a front for a crime ring?"

Robin shut off the car and turned to face her with an exaggerated grimace. "Imaginating much?"

"Well...look." Amy pointed at the sign that ran the length of the building. "Overland Protective Services. OPS for short. Like special ops."

Tracy, already facing the back seat, added her eye roll to Robin's still comical expression. "Don't make me come back there."

Even a nervous laugh was a tension breaker. Amy took a notebook and pen out of her purse and grabbed the door handle. "Okay. Let's do this." She led the way through the front door...a glass door that had been painted opaque on the inside. As if that alone wasn't suspicious.

The small waiting area was sparsely decorated with four unpadded wood chairs, a single small end table holding two magazines, and a framed black-and-white print of an arched plank door with a massive padlock. A reception desk sat at one end. There was no one in sight. Tracy and Robin sat down while Amy walked up to the desk and searched for a courtesy bell, but she couldn't find one. "Hello?"

"Be with you in a sec," a man's voice answered. Amy took a chair next to the small table and picked up a magazine. Who knew there were periodicals just for security companies? She leafed through one, scanning articles with titles like PROTECTING CRITICAL INFRASTRUCTURE INTRUSIONS WITH DEVICE-LEVEL PROTECTION and BALTIC BEVERAGE MANUFACTURER DEPLOYS SECURITY UPGRADES TO PROTECT EMPLOYEES AND ASSETS.

She heard an unseen door open, and a burly man with short reddish hair graying at the temples stepped behind the desk. "Sorry to keep you waiting. How can I help you?"

Amy pressed her hands discreetly to her sides to dry her damp palms as she stood and walked to the desk. With manufactured confidence she said, "We're hoping to speak with one of your employees. Is Emmett here?"

The man's polite smile seemed to flatten. "Emmett Mullens is no longer working for us."

Mullens. Amy tucked that bit of information away. Even if that was all they got out of this visit, it was a valuable puzzle piece. "How long ago did he leave your employ?"

The outside door opened behind her. The man's face reshaped into the welcoming smile. "Be with you in a minute," he said to the person who had entered. To Amy he said, "Let's talk in my office." He glanced toward Tracy and Robin. "They with you?" At her nod, he included them in the invitation with a wave of his hand.

The three followed him to the first door in a hallway behind the reception area. Two chairs sat in front of a desk that far surpassed Professor Douglas's in messiness. The man opened a metal folding chair and set it next to the other two. Before taking his seat, he extended his hand. "I'm Sam Wilson, owner of Overland."

Robin, Tracy, and Amy took turns introducing themselves.

"Are you clients? Did Emmett work for you?"

"No," Amy answered. A nudge in her spirit urged her to tell the man what they really wanted to know. "To be honest, Mr. Wilson, we've never met Emmett. We're worried about his girlfriend."

Mr. Wilson closed his eyes for a moment, then opened them and gave a slow nod. "Niesha." He picked up a pencil holder that had been mostly hidden by a stack of file folders. Shaped like a fist gripping pens and pencils, the holder had the now familiar dragonfly image tattooed on the wrist. "Got this in our white elephant exchange at our company Christmas party. Nice girl. Couldn't figure out what she saw in Emmett. Sorry, just being honest." His deep sigh rippled a stack of papers. "Emmett was with us for just under two years. Personality of toast, but dependable. Never had a single complaint about him until a little over a week ago. Something changed. He seemed jumpy, like he was watching over his shoulder all the time. Then he just up and stopped showing up for jobs. Had to let him go. You think Niesha is in danger? Because of him?"

"She was taking summer classes, but she's apparently dropped out of school. Her friends don't know where she is. They think she might be in some kind of danger, and..." Amy let the sentence dangle when Mr. Wilson gave what appeared to be a reluctant nod.

"I'd like to say I'd be surprised for him to do something dastardly, but I can't. Sad, though. We all thought Niesha was good for him. He seemed a bit more approachable, almost friendly, for a few weeks, then everything changed." Bushy eyebrows converged above his nose. "I overheard him talking on the phone. Might have been the last time I saw him. He asked for his paycheck a day early and he made a phone call while I was getting it ready for him. I'm sure he was talking to Niesha because he said, 'Sorry I woke you, Babe.' He kept asking her where she was staying, and he was getting pretty upset because she clearly wasn't telling him. Then he said, 'I hear the train. Bet I know where you are.' That was it. He hung up. Wish I could tell you more."

"Do you have his address?" Robin asked.

"No. A few months ago he said he'd lost his lease and was staying with friends, so he picked up his check here every week."

"Can you tell us what job sites he was working in the past few months?"

He seemed to hesitate, then stood and opened the top drawer in a tall file cabinet. "Dashel Automotive, Merten's Grocery, and the Quincy History Museum." He thumbed to another page. "And... Wolfram and Randulph Fine Arts in St. Louis."

"What?" Amy gasped. She looked at her cousin and sister and saw her shock mirrored in their faces.

Wolfram and Randulph. The gallery that had paid Grandma Pearl for *Green Girl*.

October 1, 1937

Such fun! We are hosting the church Harvest Festival right here in our backyard! Of course, Bess is going as her favorite Shirley Temple character, Elizabeth Blair. I'm not at all sure I can compete with Curly Top, but I am going as Minnie Mouse. I have leftover red and white polka-dot fabric from the skirt Grandma made me, so I will make a big bow and soak it in starch for days, and I'm going to paint my old white patent leather shoes yellow.

I saw John in town today. He caught me staring in Gamble's window and dreaming over "my" record player. He laughed when I told him all of its wonderful features. He said I should get a job at Gamble's, and I said maybe I will just do that. He also said maybe he could help me earn some money toward it, but he wouldn't tell me how. He is always so mysterious!

Anyway, I think I have convinced John to come to the festival, but he wasn't interested when he first heard about it. At first, he said he couldn't because he works a couple of days a month doing bookkeeping at his uncle's gallery in St. Louis. Then he told the truth. He didn't want to go because it made him think about the harvest festivals Hitler started in

Germany four years ago. The farmers sing and dance to celebrate the harvest, but John said it's really just to celebrate the führer. He said he can't stand to think of all the people who worship him. I think he was embarrassed for showing his anger, because he said the church festival would be a good fresh start. I tried to tell him where I live, but he said he didn't yet know the names of the streets. So I drew him a very big map on the back of a painting canvas he had in his car and told him he had to keep it forever. I guess that was a silly thing to say. Oh well, good night, dear diary!

Chapter Twelve

Amy opened one eye on Saturday morning and stared at the clock. The room was dark. Thunder rumbled, close enough to rattle the old, single-pane windows. She blinked twice as she stared at the time. How was it possible she'd slept until after seven?

Whispers floated up from downstairs. When she padded down the steps barefoot and walked through the living room, the scene in the kitchen silenced her "Good morning" before it left her lips. The table was set for three. A bouquet of black-eyed Susans filled a Mason jar in the middle. Jana, wearing pajamas and a too-big pink apron passed down from Grandma Pearl, stood in front of the sink, notepad and pencil in hand. Matt, shirtless and wearing only pajama shorts, used a spatula to gesture toward a chair. "Welcome to the M and J Café, madam."

Jana stepped forward. "Our special this morning is toast and scrambled eggs."

Amy pulled out a chair. "That sounds lovely." A glass bowl full of whipped eggs sat on the counter, but she was relieved to see Matt hadn't used the stove while she was sleeping.

Jana wrote something on her notepad. "Would you like orange juice or coffee or both?"

"Both, please." She leaned back, crossing her arms as she watched Jana take two slices of bread out of the package and stick them in the toaster. Matt turned on the stove, added a chunk of butter to the pan, then took Amy's favorite mug from the cupboard and put a coffee pod in the Keurig. "I could get used to this," she said.

With a shake of her head, Jana set a jar of strawberry jam on the table. "If you get things all the time, they aren't special."

Amy laughed. She'd said those exact words to Matt at Big O's when he'd said he wished he could eat ice cream for every meal. "Using my own words against me. Smart girl."

Matt set a steaming mug in front of Amy. "Would you like cream, ma'am?"

"I would love it. I suppose this is the kind of place where I have to leave a huge tip. If the food is as good as the service, I'll—"

Her phone, sitting next to her fork, buzzed, and she reached for it to decline the call. Nothing could be urgent enough to interrupt this time. But the name on the screen caused her breath to hitch. Lisa.

Pushing her chair back, she said, "Sorry, guys. I need to take this. It'll only take a sec." *I hope.* She stepped to the stairs, where she'd have a bit of privacy but could still keep an eye on the kitchen. "Hello. This is Amy."

"Hi. This is Lisa, Niesha's friend."

"Hi, Lisa. Do you have news?"

"I don't know. Maybe. I just found a note in a...my mailbox. From Niesha. She told me to leave a picture of a dragonfly on my website if I find out the police have arrested Emmett."

"Arrested him for what?"

"I don't know. Here, I'll read it to you. 'I'm okay. Don't worry. I'll stay in touch. Put a dragonfly on your site if they arrest him.'"

"And you're sure she meant Emmett when she said 'him'?"

"I don't know who else it would be. But here's what I wanted to tell you. I have genetic hyperosmia, this really crazy sense of smell. Niesha's letter smelled like smoke."

"Cigarette smoke?" Amy had no idea how that information would be helpful.

"No. Like campfire smoke. She's backpacked all over the country. I think she might be camping."

"Does she ever camp near railroad tracks?"

"Not that I know of. Unless…there's that little campground down by the river, but I think she'd want to be far away from Canton if she's running from Emmett. Why?"

Amy explained what they'd learned from Sam Wilson. "What kind of vehicle does she drive?"

"She has a red car. I don't know what kind it is. There's a smiley face bumper sticker on the back."

"Okay. Thank you. This all helps."

"Should I tell the police about the smoke?"

"Definitely. And I'll talk to Pastor Gary. I know he's taken youth groups backpacking in the past. Maybe he has some ideas. If you hear anything else, please let me know."

"I will. And thanks for praying for her."

"My privilege. I'm praying for you too, Lisa."

"Thanks. Bye."

Amy closed her eyes for a moment, listening to the rain pelting the porch roof, trying to regain the joy she'd had walking into the kitchen. She'd read the book that claimed women were like spaghetti and men were like waffles. At the moment, she wished she could compartmentalize her thoughts into nice, neat waffle squares instead of the spaghetti tangle winding through her brain. She had to try. Matt and Jana deserved her full attention.

She stopped and took several pictures of the two hard at work, then, with a smile, she went back to her seat and gushed over fluffy eggs and perfectly browned toast. Matt and Jana sat at the table, and they joined hands. For the first time ever, Matt offered to pray without being asked.

"Dear God, thank You for this food and for letting us surprise Mom. Please help whoever was on the phone and show us how to solve the mystery of the painting. Amen."

Amy's voice was tight as she echoed her son. "Amen."

The surprises continued when Matt and Jana ordered her to relax on the porch swing while they cleaned up the kitchen. After texting Tracy and Robin about the call from Lisa—and pictures of the precious miracle taking place in her kitchen—Amy checked Niesha's social media accounts, hoping to find clues, but there were no new posts. She tapped on the URL for Niesha's website and scrolled through pictures of her pottery creations. Nothing new. When she'd first seen the website, she'd only looked at the pottery, not Niesha's other artwork, so she tapped on the tab labeled PAINTINGS.

The girl was gifted. Dozens of watercolors filled the page like a patchwork quilt. Flowers, trees, covered bridges, mountains, waterfalls. The Gateway Arch reflected in the river. The Chain of Rocks Bridge. Several paintings captured the grounds and buildings of

Culver-Stockton College. Views of the Mississippi from the bluffs. And then, a blob of bright yellow caught her attention. A tent, nestled in a valley at the base of a mountain. The next painting seemed to be a close-up of the same picture. Worn hiking boots leaned against a backpack next to the yellow tent. A campfire burned not far away.

Though the scene was in the mountains, far from Canton, it may have given them an important clue. A yellow pup tent.

Jumping up, she yelled to the kids, "Let's go for a ride! I need to check out something that might be a clue to our mystery, and then I'm going to treat the M and J Café crew to a rainy-day movie."

Jana squealed and Matt fist-pumped. "Mystery and a movie!" he yelled as he ran up the stairs to get dressed. "I'll get my camera. The supersleuths are gonna solve this thing!"

Though heavy pewter-gray clouds still hung low over the Mississippi, the rain had slowed to a sporadic *drip-drip-drip*. Amy made a sharp turn onto Front Street at Washington Park. Three linked-together barges crept up the river. Just beyond them, on the Illinois side, the feed silos of the Farmers Co-op in Warsaw stood like silver silhouettes against the leaden sky.

Sixteen diagonal campsites lined the road, about twenty feet from the river. Beyond them, a small pavilion and a playground offered picnic space on a nicer day. Amy scanned the campsites. Only five were filled. Two travel trailers, a pop-up camper, and two tents. Neither of them yellow.

"She's not here, is she?" Matt asked from the back seat. Amy had filled him in with just the barest details, asking both of the kids to pray for Niesha.

"It doesn't look like it." Just then, a woman with a small, fluffy dog on a leash stepped out of one of the campers. "Stay in the car. I'm going to go talk to her." She turned to make eye contact, making sure her command was heard. They both nodded.

Waving as she walked toward the gray-haired woman, Amy called, "Nice day for a walk, huh?"

The woman laughed. "I tried telling Cleopatra here that she didn't really need to go out now." As if understanding her words, the dog squatted in the wet grass.

"I don't want to keep you, but I'm looking for someone. A friend of mine, a young woman with a yellow tent. Have you seen—"

The woman started nodding before Amy finished her sentence. "Natalie. Sweet girl. She packed up early this morning before the rain started."

Natalie? Was she talking about someone else, or had the woman forgotten her name? Or was Niesha using a different name? That made the most sense.

"Dark skin, curly hair?"

"That's the one. Cleopatra loved her, and she doesn't take to just anyone. She's a good judge of character. The girl did seem a bit skittish. I asked her why she was camping alone, and she said she was looking for an apartment. We got the feeling maybe she had money problems. My husband slipped a fifty under the visor in her car when she wasn't looking. He loves to do that kind of stuff."

Amy's hand splayed against her chest. It was a gesture she couldn't remember using before becoming a foster mom. "That's so kind of you. My pastor and I are worried about her. We think her boyfriend might be causing trouble for her. Did she have any visitors that you know of?"

"Not that I saw, but that explains a lot. Every time I talked to her, I got the feeling she was looking over my shoulder, waiting for someone. Poor thing."

"Did she mention where she was going?"

The woman's lips puckered, and her eyes narrowed. "She said she was going to do some hiking. She told my husband she makes pottery and was going to a place where she could dig her own clay. Oh! And look for geodes." She shrugged. "I don't know if that helps."

"It might. I'll have to ask someone who knows more about geology than I do." She thanked the woman and ran back toward the car just as the rain started again in earnest.

"Wait!"

Amy stopped and turned, shielding her eyes from the downpour.

"I think she threw her phone in the river. I saw her talking on it and then she pitched something at the water. Pretty sure it was her phone."

"Thank you so much. You've been very helpful."

"We'll be praying for—" A tug from Cleopatra cut off her statement.

Amy dashed to the car and slid in, shaking water from her hair and raincoat.

"Does she know where Niesha is?" Matt rested his chin on the back of the passenger seat.

"She doesn't know where she is, but she said she was going someplace where she could hike and dig for her own clay and look for geodes. Any idea where that would be?"

"Hmm. Nope. I bet Uncle Jeff would know. He collects rocks and stuff."

"Good point." Jeff the history buff was building an entire wall of shelves in his home office for displaying his metal-detecting finds and rock collection. "We'll go talk to him after the movie."

Before they left the campground, Amy called Lisa and told her what she'd learned, then said, "Your heightened sense of smell comes in pretty handy."

"Sometimes. People get tired of me pointing out things they can't smell, but mostly it's good. I can sniff out a dead mouse in the walls better than my cat."

Amy grimaced. "Well, see, it's a gift."

"Hey, I left a message for Niesha. I told her someone named Angel was helping me find her and she could trust you."

"I'm…Angel?"

"Yeah. You are to me. Anyway, if you do find her, that's your code name. Kind of dramatic, I guess, but I don't think we can be too careful."

"I agree." Again, she reminded Lisa she was praying, then they said goodbye.

As she drove, Amy considered how she'd answer Tracy's inevitable "What do we do next?" question. In truth, she was relieved they'd hit a dead end with finding Emmett. Robin had called the police to tell them what they'd learned at the security company. That was a trail best followed by those who were equipped to handle what could be a volatile situation. Focusing on finding Niesha seemed to be the best way they could help and not hinder.

She sighed as they crossed the Quincy Memorial Bridge for the second time in two days. Were they getting in over their heads? This quest was taking up a lot of time. What had started as mere curiosity had morphed into a search for a girl who could be in danger. The stakes were so much higher than simply unraveling how Green Girl had traveled over three and a half decades from Grandma Pearl's house to a flea market in St. Louis. This felt like a calling, a mission they needed to see through to the end.

There, she'd talked herself back into it.

"I think," came a voice from the back seat, "we need to go camping so we can find her. Do we have a tent?"

Camping? She hadn't done that in years. But how could she resist any suggestion from a ten-year-old boy for "we" time?

"We don't have a tent, but I bet somebody in the family does. And maybe it's time we start collecting our own camping equipment. What do you think, Jana, sound fun?" She glanced over her shoulder and laughed at the little girl gawking at her brother across the back seat.

"Camping?" Jana squeaked. "Outside? With bugs and bears and...at night?"

"Duh," Matt answered. "You're such a girl."

Amy stifled another laugh as they pulled into the theater parking lot. "Someday, my son, girls being girls won't seem like such an awful thing."

Chapter Thirteen

Rain pelted the bare upstairs windows in the stripped-down room where Jeff was working on Saturday afternoon. He'd brushed off two five-gallon buckets of drywall mud for Amy and Matt to sit on. Trowel in hand, he crouched, leaning his back against the doorframe and listened to their questions.

"Can't comprehend why anyone would want to dig for their own when you can order a chunk of clean clay online, but I guess it's all part of the artist thing I just don't get." Jeff slid dust-covered goggles onto the top of his head. "Anyway, there's a place near Alexandria. I went up with a buddy of mine last summer hunting geodes, and there were two people digging in the mud along the river and hauling it to their truck in buckets. Being the nosy kind, I asked what they were doing and found out they were owners of a pottery shop. They said they preferred to process their own clay and some of the best in the country was found right there."

"Cool," Matt said. "I bet Niesha is there."

Jeff looked down, half hiding an amused smile. "There are a lot of campgrounds in the area. I hate to be a downer, but I think your chances of finding her are pretty slim."

Matt shook his head. "All we have to do is drive around every campground and look for a yellow tent."

Amy covered her grimace with a hand over her face. She locked eyes with her brother-in-law, and they shared a moment of mirth.

"So you need camping stuff, huh?" Jeff winked at Amy. "Nothing like sleeping on the hard ground to make a person feel young again." He stood and put his hand on Matt's shoulder. "Guess we better go do some treasure hunting in the garage while the womenfolk are doing their thing in the attic."

Matt jumped up. "Seriously? Now?"

"Sure."

"You should come camping with us!" Matt looked at Jeff with hope-filled puppy dog eyes.

A laugh like a popping balloon burst from Jeff. He looked at Amy. "How do you ever say no to this guy?"

"I don't. Not often enough anyway."

"Huh," Matt puffed out, then turned to Jeff. "My friend Blake got a jackknife for his birthday, but Mom doesn't think *I'm* old enough."

Jeff tousled Matt's hair. "I used to think my mother was just trying to spoil my fun when she said no. It wasn't until I was a lot older that I realized she always had a good reason. Moms can be pretty smart sometimes."

Matt shrugged. "Yeah. Sometimes, anyways."

Jeff laughed. "Come on, kiddo. Let's dodge the raindrops and go find some camping stuff." Turning to Amy he said, "Talk to Tracy about going. Unless we wait for the weekend, and I'm guessing you won't want to, I have classes, but I'd be happy to make the commute."

They left on their treasure hunting expedition in the garage, and Amy joined Tracy and Jana in the attic.

Tracy greeted her with, "Do you want all of this?" She sat on the floor surrounded by open boxes and crumpled newspaper. Arranged in front of her was a fanciful array of green Depression glass.

"Yes!" Amy checked on Jana, who'd found an old wicker doll buggy and had put all of her wooden "babies" in it, then joined Tracy on the floor. "I just decided I want to paint my kitchen a lighter shade of this." She held a shallow bowl up to the light. "I'm going to take the doors off all the top cabinets, the ones I can't reach anyway, and use them for display."

"Love it. Jeff can help you install lights in them. Can't you imagine your kitchen glowing green at night?"

Amy gave a dreamy sigh. "Are you sure you and Robin don't want any of these?" She pulled another wrapped piece from a box.

"We've had decades of collecting stuff while you've been living the minimalist life we both want."

It was true. She wasn't a saver. Half her kitchen cupboards were still empty, even though she'd already taken some of Grandma's dishes and pots and pans, but she had a feeling that would change by the time they finished sorting through the attic. She unwrapped a narrow bud vase and set it on the floor. As she did, she noticed something in the bottom of a covered candy dish. She lifted the top and pulled out a small, slightly yellowed envelope, about three inches square with *Pearly* written in blue ink. Inside was a card with several lines scrawled in back-slanted cursive. "'December 25, 1938. Because green is your color. Sorry I couldn't top last year's gift. Have a fabulous birthday. Love, JW.'" She handed it to Tracy. "Didn't we find a picture of Grandma with someone named JW?"

"Maybe. All these names, dates, and faces are becoming a blur." Tracy swept her hand over the glass displayed in front of them. "Green definitely was Grandma's color."

"She wore a lot of green, didn't—" Amy stopped and stared at Tracy. She took the card back, opened it again, and tapped the handwritten message. "It says 1938. So whatever JW gave her for her birthday in 1937 was better than a candy dish." She felt the effects of adrenaline pumping through her veins. "I can't make sense of this yet, but we assume Grandma got money for Green Girl on her birthday in 1937. What if we've had this all wrong? What if *she* painted it? What if the birthday gift was a big check? What if the W stands for Wolfram?"

Tracy met her question with a blank stare. "So the gallery paid her for the painting…and then let her keep it?"

"I don't know. Maybe. What if they bought it from her and then she bought it back later? Or her parents bought it? Or something." Her voice faded as the ridiculousness of her theory became clearer.

"It's not impossible," Tracy said, obviously trying to placate her. "But if we're right that the same artist painted the castle picture, Grandma would have done that one when she was like fourteen. Still not impossible. Though we never saw any other evidence of her being interested in painting."

Feeling more foolish by the minute, Amy picked up another stack of pictures and pretended to be fascinated by them. In truth, her thoughts were stuck on the mysterious JW.

Robin joined them in the attic after she closed the store. Amy looked up from going through a stack of photographs she'd sorted days ago into a bag labeled *1960s*. After Tracy showed Robin the note, Amy said, "I know I saw 'JW' on the back of another picture." She racked her over-full brain. "I remember it was from the sixties because at first I thought Grandma was wearing hippie braids. Ah! I remember. She was wearing a Dorothy costume and Grandpa was the Tin Man. 'JW' was dressed like the scarecrow." She flipped through a dozen more pictures then gave a triumphant shout. "Got it!" Tracy and Robin moved in close, one on each side of her.

Holding the photograph close to her eyes, she examined the man. He was at least six inches taller than Grandma. A mass of straw covered his head, so she couldn't see his hair color. He wore a silver band on his left hand. "Grandma's maiden name was Wallace," Amy said. "Could he be a relative?"

Tracy shrugged one shoulder. "Her brother was killed in Korea, so it couldn't be him. Possibly a cousin, I suppose."

Amy took the photo and looked at the back. "Whether they were friends or family, they would have known each other for decades at this point." She flipped it over again and held it inches from her nose.

"I'll ask Mom about him," Robin said. She leaned closer to the picture. "Hey. This was taken at the church harvest party. I had no idea that's been going on so long."

Amy felt a jolt. It was a sensation she should be used to by now. Some would call it a light bulb moment. For her, it was the feeling of another puzzle piece slipping into place. She held up one finger. "We need to find out if the church keeps records that go back that far."

"Good thought," Robin said. "And speaking of old records, one of us needs to call the gallery in St. Louis."

"And Jeff knows a place near Alexandria where Niesha may have gone looking for geodes and clay." Amy glanced at the window. "I'd drive up there right now and look around if it wasn't storming. I can't go tomorrow because of Jana's visitation. But Matt has a plan."

When Robin gave her a questioning look, she told them about their conversation with Jeff and how Matt's eyes had lit when he talked about a family campout. "I think Monday might be unrealistic. We'd need time to shop and pack. I guess I'll plan on taking the kids up on Tuesday. Would either of you want to join us?" It was asking a lot, she knew, so she tried to tamp down her hopes.

Robin shoved her bangs aside. "Kai would love that. And I suppose I could survive a couple of nights in a tent. I think we still have one somewhere."

"Sounds like Jeff committed us," Tracy said, "so I guess I'm in. I can finish up a couple of articles on Monday, so Eric should be good with it."

"Thanks, guys. This will be fun." Amy's smile felt tight, even though she was genuinely grateful. She knew their chances of finding Niesha diminished with each passing day.

"Tell you what." Tracy slipped her arm across Amy's shoulders. "Jeff and I will drive up tomorrow afternoon and try to find a couple of campsites and look around for a yellow tent while we're at it."

"You'd do that?" Amy wrapped her arms around her sister. "You're the best."

Pastor Gary preached about depending on God for strength. He started the service with the preschool class singing "Jesus Loves Me." Emerson, standing in the middle of the front row of more than a dozen children, rolled and unrolled the front of her skirt while staring straight ahead and not singing a word. Wisely, her mama had dressed her in bright pink leggings beneath the sparkly flounces. Big brother made up for her silence. Corbin's voice rose above the rest as he sang with gusto, almost on key. Amy alternated between watching them and sneaking looks at Jeff and Tracy, who were beaming with the kind of pride Amy was beginning to understand firsthand.

When the children paraded back to their class, Pastor Gary said, "'We are weak, but He is strong.' Anyone feeling weak today?"

Amy joined most of the congregation by raising her hand, then opened her Bible to the passage in Isaiah and read along with Pastor Gary. "'So do not fear, for I am with you; do not be dismayed, for I am your God. I will strengthen you and help you; I will uphold you with my righteous right hand.'"

More words worth memorizing. Through the rest of the message, she tried to grasp the concept that weakness was actually a good thing, that admitting she couldn't do life on her own wasn't failure, but freedom. He ended with, "Let's all say it out loud. Repeat after me: I can't."

The two words echoed off the walls as more than two hundred people said, "I can't."

"Now let's follow it up with another truth." He pointed heavenward. "God can!"

Goose bumps skipped along her arms as she joined the chorus of voices. He was right. There was freedom in knowing the Lord would be her strength. All the strength she would need to get through this afternoon's visitation.

After the service, Terry and Jeff took Kai, Matt, and Jana to pick up the sub sandwiches from Café Chew they'd enjoy on Terry and Robin's rooftop terrace above the store. The women stayed behind to talk to Pastor Gary.

When the line of worshipers had finally trickled out, Amy approached him. First, she told him everything they'd learned about Emmett and Niesha, then asked him if he had ever taken his current college Bible study group camping or backpacking.

"Not yet, but we have a trip planned for September. I told them about taking our high school youth to Ha Ha Tonka State Park, and Niesha was the one who suggested we plan a trip there for the college group." He rubbed his hand over his chin. "Come to think of it, she volunteered to check out the Turkey Pen Hollow Trail sometime before we go so that we'd know just what to expect."

Robin gave a loud sigh. "One more place to look."

Amy shared the frustration. Ha Ha Tonka was the opposite direction from Alexandria. They couldn't possibly check out every lead. Unless they split up. Still, that was too far away just to drive around looking for a yellow tent. It made far more sense to search the area around the clay pit less than half an hour north of Canton. She shook herself out of her heavy thoughts and looked at Pastor Gary. "One more thing. We found a picture of a man whose initials are JW. We think he might have been connected to our painting. It's likely he attended church here in the sixties. Does the church keep membership records going back that far?"

Pastor Gary's eyes brightened. "We have records going all the way back to the *eighteen* sixties when the church was built. Stop by the office anytime this week and have a look." He rubbed his hands together. "This is exciting."

His enthusiasm was contagious. They thanked him and talked over each other all the way out of the church. The weight Amy had carried on her shoulders when she arrived an hour and a half earlier had been lifted. She walked out into the sunlit, rain-washed day with a smile. "Who's hungry for subs? I hope they don't forget the kettle chips. Matt loves—"

Her words jammed in her throat. Coming around the corner across the street was a black SUV with a crumpled front fender and a headlight that bobbed like a blinking eyeball.

October 16, 1937

Sorry I was too tired to write last night after Bess and I saw Mr. Dodd Takes the Air at the Gem. We laughed so hard! After the movie, we decided we are going to pluck our eyebrows exactly like Jane Wyman's. She is so beautiful, and she is only four years older than I am.

It was a gorgeous day today. The sky was azure blue (I love the word azure!) and there were patches of color on the trees along the river. Bess and I went for a bicycle ride and stopped at the Coffee Shop for chocolate sodas. She had to be home for her father's birthday at two, but I wasn't ready to go home yet, so I rode over to Richard's house. He was still helping his father plant bushes, so I got brave and went to John's house. Their housekeeper answered the door. She wore a black uniform with a white apron. She has a very strong German accent. She said "Yon" would be with me in a minute and told me to wait in the foyer.

None of my friends have housekeepers! The Wolfs must be very rich. Curiosity got the best of me, so I walked a couple of steps beyond the foyer just to look around. Their house is so beautiful. The floors are as shiny as mirrors and there's a giant chandelier in the hallway with crystal teardrops hanging from it. There are gold candelabras on the fireplace mantel like I've seen in pictures of castles in Europe.

The housekeeper walked through a narrow door under the stairway. It didn't have a frame around it, like it was supposed to be invisible. I stepped back because I got the feeling I wasn't supposed to see it, but I peeked around the wall in the foyer and saw John come out of that door following the housekeeper and close it behind him. It really did disappear. If you didn't know it was there, you would never see it. I returned to the front door before he saw me, so he doesn't know I know about the secret door.

He acted strange. We never have a hard time coming up with things to say, but today was different. We sat on padded chairs with gold-painted wood, and the housekeeper brought us glasses of iced tea. We talked about the weather, and he said Gänse and her family will be getting on an ocean liner in a week. Mr. Wolf found a house for them here in Canton. John said Gänse's father is his mentor. He is an artist too. He acted happy about them coming, but I think he is very worried for their safety. Father read about a museum exhibit that will open soon in Munich. It is all about how bad the Jewish people are. I want to ask John about it. Does he know any Jewish people? What does he think of them? Does he think there will be another big war?

I have so many questions, but right now the biggest one is what is behind the secret door and how can I find out?

Good night, dear diary.

Chapter Fourteen

"You're sure?" Tracy handed Amy a cup of tea. Even though the thermometer on Robin's rooftop terrace nudged ninety, she claimed hot tea was the only antidote for nerves.

"One hundred percent." Amy blew on the steaming amber brew in the china cup. "And the driver did the exact same thing in front of our house. Slowed down and then sped up. It was too dark to see inside the car the first time, and this time I was so focused on the wobbly headlight, I didn't think to look at the driver until it was pulling away."

Robin patted her hand. "We need to call the police."

"And tell them what? We saw the same vehicle that drove past my house a few days ago in front of our church this morning? That was probably true of twenty cars parked in the parking lot."

"You and the kids stay here tonight," Robin said. "Terry will insist on it."

"Good luck with that." Tracy took a strawberry from the fruit tray in the center of the picnic table. "We tried getting her to stay with us after we saw Emmett in Matt's video."

"She's always been stubborn like that."

"Tell me about it."

Amy kept her eyes on Kai teaching Matt how to use his homemade bubble cannon to launch giant bubbles onto Main Street and tried not to laugh as her sister and cousin carried on, attempting to get a rise out of her.

"Remember that time Grandma Pearl took us to St. Louis for the weekend and we went to the Old Spaghetti Factory, but Amy wanted Taco Bell, so she refused to eat." Robin poked Amy's arm for emphasis on the last three words.

"The best pasta and garlic bread in the whole world, and she went to bed hungry. Then she woke me up at midnight whining because she was *staaaaarving*."

"She's just like that. Stubborn. Stubborn. Stubborn." Again, the arm pokes from Robin. "Wasn't that the same weekend we went to the history museum and she wanted to spend the whole day looking at the dollhouse and she wouldn't budge from—"

"I. Was. Eight!" Amy laughed, causing tea to splash onto the jabbing finger. "Serves you right," she said, wiping the splatter off Robin's hand.

Tracy doled out napkins. "Pull it together, ladies." She was laughing just as hard as the other two. "This is serious business."

Amy fanned her face with a napkin. "What I seriously need right now is this. Laughter is the best medicine, and I could use a cure before I leave." She glanced at Robin. "You're sure it's okay if Matt stays?"

"You know you don't even have to ask." She pointed to the corner of the brick wall that surrounded the deck. Kai was dipping a giant ring made from a wire coat hanger into his "secret special bubble sauce" and making Jana laugh as "elephant bubbles" drifted out over the town and Rocket, Terry and Robin's Australian shepherd, stood on his hind legs trying to snap at them. "I don't have many regrets in life, but I do wish I could have given that boy a sibling or two. This is so good for him."

They sat in silence for several minutes, watching the bubble-blowing crew. Amy finished her tea, then extricated one leg at a time from the picnic table bench.

"Let's pray before you go, okay?" Tracy didn't wait for an answer. Taking Amy's hand, she prayed for Amy, Jana, Janelle, and Dillon, asking God for whatever was best for the children. When she finished, Robin prayed that not being included in this visit wouldn't affect Matt.

"Amen." Amy dabbed her damp lashes with a napkin. "Matt seemed to take it pretty well. More than feeling left out, I think he's worried about Jana. He doesn't have a high opinion of Dillon. I gather he was out of their lives more than in when he and Janelle were together."

"This is all so hard," Robin said as she stood. "But we have to believe God's got this all figured out." She yelled to Terry, who sidled over to them. "Would you please go down and scope out the street before Amy and Jana get in their car?" she asked.

"Anything for the women in my life." Terry gave Amy a one-armed hug. "Are you sure you don't want one of us to go with you?"

"I'm sure. I'm taking Jana out for supper after the visit. We need some girl time. You're doing enough by watching Matt."

"Hey, that's purely selfish. This is keeping our boy off his mind-numbing electronics." He squeezed her shoulder again, then headed inside, leaving Amy with a roller coaster of mixed feelings. She couldn't possibly be more grateful for the protectiveness of her family, yet she hated burdening them with the need to be her bodyguards. Between the highs of gratitude and the dips of guilt were the sheer drops of fear. Had Emmett Mullens found her? If so, what did he want? Should she stay away from Jeff and Tracy's house to avoid leading him to the painting? Had he followed her here? Were her children safe? Those questions led her right back to this afternoon's meeting.

As she called to Jana, words from the morning's message ran like a scrolling marquis through her churning thoughts.

So do not fear, for I am with you; do not be dismayed, for I am your God. I will strengthen you and help you; I will uphold you with my righteous right hand.

"A dollar for your thoughts," Amy prodded as she glanced at Jana in the rearview mirror.

Hugging the stuffed Piglet Amy had given her the first time they'd met, Jana looked up with wide, sad eyes. "I'm kinda scared."

"I know, baby. That's normal. You haven't seen Dillon in a long time." She couldn't bring herself to say "your father." Maybe that was wrong. Maybe he really was a changed man. At the very least, she needed to give him the benefit of the doubt. She'd work on that while sitting in the car and waiting for the ordeal to be over. "What scares you the most?"

Burying her face in pink fur, Jana gave a quiet, muffled answer. "Matt said Melanie might make us go back to Mama."

Amy took two slow, measured breaths. "You know it's Melanie's job to make sure you and Matt are safe and happy, right? Before any big decisions like that get made, she's going to talk to you and let you ask questions and check everything out. And today, if anything makes you afraid, you just grab her hand. I'll tell her that's our sign. Okay?"

Dark curls bounced as Jana nodded.

"There's a difference between being nervous and being afraid of something that's really scary. Most people feel jittery when they don't know what's going to happen. When I walk into my classroom for the first time next month, I'm going to be nervous."

That got Jana's attention. "But you're a grown-up."

Amy smiled in the mirror. "Yep. That doesn't matter. I haven't met my class yet. I don't know if they'll like me or if I'll have some kids who don't want to follow the rules. It's not something really scary, because I know I'll be safe, but it still makes me nervous. So if you're feeling butterflies in your stomach, that's perfectly normal."

A giggle from the back seat allowed Amy to lower her shoulders as she flipped on the turn signal. "What's so funny?"

"You. Scared of first graders."

"Go ahead and laugh, Peanut." She would have put on a clown nose and a blaze-orange wig and stood on her head on Main Street just to hear that sound.

But Jana's smile disappeared the moment Amy put the car in park. Amy scrambled to get it back. "I already sent in our order for Breadeaux in Palmyra. Cheeseburger pizza. Add bacon, hold the onion, easy on the Dijon, just like you like it."

"With dill pickles?" Jana's tiny voice squeaked.

"Extra dill pickles. We'll pick it up and go to Flower City Park. Sound fun?"

Jana's nod was barely perceptible. "You're going to stay here, right?"

"I'm not going anywhere."

Only one car was parked in the gravel space just wide enough for three vehicles. The park was really just a triangle of grass with two picnic tables, a trash can, and a green plastic outhouse with SCOTTIES POTTIES written on the side.

Melanie got out of her car, carrying a tablet and a small stuffed bear. Pooh Bear. Amy didn't have to turn around to know Jana was smiling. Melanie, in her late twenties, was passionate about her calling. Her care for "her" kids was genuine.

They met in front of Amy's car. When Melanie held out the bear, Jana squealed and spontaneously hugged her around the waist. The look of surprise on Melanie's face as she wrapped her arms around Jana was priceless. She mouthed "Progress?" with raised eyebrows, and Amy nodded and gave a thumbs-up. So much progress. How much of it would get undone today?

"Any questions, Jana?" Melanie asked.

"Uh-huh. I can still go home with my mom today, can't I?"

Amy answered Melanie's subtle look of question by discreetly pointing to herself as she silently formed the words "I'm Mom."

"You will absolutely go home with your mom today. If any changes are going to be made, I promise we will talk about it first. No surprises, okay?"

Amy knew enough about Melanie's job to know that "promise" and "no surprises" weren't words she got to use often. She told Melanie about their "sign," and she agreed. "I'll be close enough so you can squeeze my hand," she assured. "Mom…" She looked at Amy and her expression said she understood the unspoken fear. "Any questions?"

"None right now." Amy hugged Jana, got back into the car, and turned up the AC and the radio. She'd wanted to say so much more, but she didn't trust her voice. If this was just a visit with Jana's biological parents, if so much didn't hang in the balance, she would have encouraged her to enjoy this time. If Janelle had never said she was ready to relinquish her rights, this would have been easier. Maybe.

She'd been coached by Melanie before the kids came to live with her. She'd attended classes and meetings and read everything she could get her hands on. She could write her own book using all the great advice she'd read on blogs or been given by other foster parents. *It's not about "getting" a child, it's about giving yourself to a child. It's not about you. Let go of the fear of having to say goodbye and replace it with the fear of a child growing up without ever knowing the kind of love you have to give. That vulnerability you're scared of is the one thing some child needs the most. If you're afraid of getting too attached, you're the right person for the job.*

A maroon sedan pulled up. Janelle was driving. She exited the car, stomped out a cigarette, and started walking toward the picnic table where Jana sat with Melanie. A few minutes later, a man in a Hawaiian shirt and khaki pants got out of the passenger side. He slammed the door harder than necessary, then took long strides across the grass. Amy only got a quick glance before he started walking toward the others, but the family resemblance was obvious.

Sliding her seat back as far as it would go, she closed her eyes. She didn't have to watch. Maybe she'd take a short nap. Two seconds later, her eyes popped open. She needed to stay awake and pray. She watched Janelle bend and engulf Jana in a hug that had to feel smothering, and Amy quickly closed her eyes again. Just then, her phone rang. Robin. Once again, her timing was perfect.

"Hi, Rob." In the next second, another thought flashed like ambulance lights. "Is Matt okay?"

"He's fine. Chad came over with Corbin. Matt's putting on a bubble show for him. I got a video for you. It's adorable. Are you at the park? Everything all right?"

"Everything's okay."

"Good. Got a minute to talk?"

"Yes." She hadn't even started to pray, but God had answered one of her needs. "Distract me."

"Gladly. Jeff and Tracy just left, and I had to fill you in on what we found out."

"You have my attention."

Robin gave a low laugh. "So it seems we have a support team."

"For what?" Amy glanced at the foursome huddled together in the middle of the green space in front of her, then shifted sideways, away from the other cars, with a view of a mobile home park.

"Our mystery. Tracy got a call from Grace. She and Columbia have been chatting about Green Girl and came up with a theory."

Amy sat up straighter. "A theory of who painted it? Or who stole it?"

"Who stole it," Robin said. "Columbia dug out some of her notes from May of 1987. She had several pages about things Grandma and

Elizabeth did together while Elizabeth was visiting. One thing she'd noted was an argument they'd had over a 'gentleman friend.'"

"'Gentleman friend'?" Amy laughed. "She thought they were fighting over a man? They were in their sixties!"

"Hey. Be careful. That doesn't sound so old from where I'm standing."

"Sorry. That was inconsiderate." So was the laugh she tacked on to the comment. "Please tell me Columbia didn't put that in her column. Could the man have been JW?"

"That's what I wondered too, but Columbia couldn't remember his name. And, no, she didn't put it in the paper. Anyway, Columbia talked to Grace and together they did some research. Elizabeth died in 2015. She grew up in Canton, went to college in Indiana, then, sometime in the forties, got a job in Chicago. She had a younger sister, Lucille Morgan. Lucille is eighty-four. Here's where it gets interesting. In 2013 Elizabeth went to live with Lucille. In St. Louis! Which means all of her prized possessions would have moved with her, right? Now, Lucille is on a waiting list for a prestigious assisted living home. Which means she has to be downsizing, right?"

Amy rubbed her right temple. "They're thinking Elizabeth stole the painting from her best friend? Why?"

"Revenge."

"Wow. So she stole it, reported it to the police herself, kept it in Chicago, then moved it to St. Louis and now…what? Lucille gave it to Niesha to sell at the flea market?"

"Yes. Or something close to that."

Why wouldn't Lucille sell it outright? Because she was afraid of someone uncovering the truth? Why would Elizabeth steal from her best friend? Amy squeezed her eyes shut. There wasn't room in her worry-filled brain for more questions. "Isn't that a bit of a stretch?"

"No!" Excitement fizzed in Tracy's voice. "Because... Drum roll, please. The house Elizabeth grew up in is on the corner of Eighth and Lewis."

A gasp slipped from Amy's lips. "One of the houses marked on the map on the back of Green Girl."

Chapter Fifteen

Sweet tea in hand, Amy sat on the porch swing, listening to night sounds and trying to clear her mind. Next to her on the swing sat the baby monitor she hadn't used since the first week they'd lived there. At bedtime, Jana had been clingy, asking Amy to read book after book for nearly an hour. Though clearly exhausted, she fought sleep, probably afraid of having another nightmare.

Jana had been quiet on the way home, and Amy hadn't pried. Melanie said she hadn't talked much, simply nodding, shaking her head, or shrugging when Janelle peppered her with questions. Dillon hadn't said more than ten words. It was clear to Melanie they'd been fighting. Amy tried to repent of the feeling of hope that gave her, but the hope was tempered by the apparent change in Melanie's opinion of Dillon Rundel. She now thought he was really a good guy who'd had a lot of bad breaks. "He started turning his life around, but a year ago his parents were severely injured in a car accident, and he gave up his job to be their full-time caregiver. Now he has a new job and is working hard to change his ways." Though Amy genuinely felt sorry for the man, Melanie's defense of him scared her.

Her phone buzzed with a call from Tracy. Amy answered the same way she had for decades. "Hey, Sis."

"How did it go today?"

"You tell me first. Any sign of Niesha?"

"Sorry, no. We checked out three campgrounds and made reservations for three nights at Cliffside Park. It was the only place we could get two sites together, and some of the tent sites are so secluded we couldn't get a good look at them. So she could still be there."

Amy smiled at her sister's offer of hope. "Thank you for doing this."

"It was a nice way to spend the day together. Now tell me about the visit."

Amy recapped what she knew of the visitation and told her about Jana's restlessness at bedtime.

"Poor thing. This has to be so confusing. On some level she must be torn. How are you doing?"

Amy ran a hand through tangled hair. The wind had picked up while they were sharing pizza in the park. She hadn't even glanced in the mirror since she got home. She must look a fright. "I'm ashamed to admit I'm glad Janelle and Dillon weren't getting along. I know that sounds selfish. I want to believe I'd be happy for the kids if they had a stable family to go back to. I just can't see this being a good situation."

"Matt asked us to pray with him at four o'clock."

"What?" Her eyes smarted with instant tears. "*He* asked you?"

"Yep. You can be so proud of that kid. We all gathered on the terrace and held hands and prayed."

Amy couldn't stop the sob that shook her shoulders. Tracy waited in silence. After a minute, Amy squeezed out a hoarse, "They can't go back."

"God knows. That always sounds so trite, but it's true."

"He does." Amy looked up at a sky peppered with stars.

"Tell me you don't have plans for tomorrow. Your self-appointed distractors made some phone calls tonight."

"Okay. Nothing important going on tomorrow."

"Good. We're planning to see Elizabeth's sister, Lucille, at her house, followed by a visit to Wolfram & Randulph Fine Arts and lunch at Stacked."

Though she'd consumed half a pizza just two hours earlier, Amy's mouth watered at the thought of the burger bar that specialized in "build your own" creations. The last time they were there, she created a masterpiece their server had jokingly said they would name after her: grass-fed beef on a pretzel bun topped with feta cheese, grilled pineapple, caramelized onions, and strawberry maple jam. "You don't have to ask me twice."

"Good. After lunch we're going to hit up an army surplus store."

"Stocking up on MREs?" The few times Grandma had served Grandpa corned beef hash or stew out of a can, he'd said they reminded him too much of the army-issued "meals ready to eat."

Tracy laughed. "Camping supplies."

"Oh. Right." There was a time in her life when the last thing in the world she wanted was having decisions made for her. Especially by the big sister who thought she was supposed to step into the mom role after their parents died. Today, Amy was nothing but grateful for her take-charge family. "That all sounds wonderful."

They chatted a bit longer, then Amy resumed unwinding from the day. After opening her phone to the Green Girl Mystery file, she added Lucille Morgan. Would she know anything? If Elizabeth had stolen the painting, would she have told her sister? Maybe a deathbed confession? It was possible that this part of their mystery could be solved tomorrow. Columbia and Grace's theory stretched the boundaries of belief, but stranger things had happened. Like finding Green Girl at a flea market.

She hadn't checked Niesha's website or social media in a couple of days. Nothing on nieshadoesart.com. She tapped to Instagram. Nothing new. She scrolled down, taking her time to study the photographs taken by a woman with a true eye for beauty. Sunsets, waterfalls, butterflies, and dozens of pottery creations.

Then, something caught her eye. She halted the slow movement of the swing and studied a photograph of a woman's hand holding a cut geode. A triangle of crystals sparkled in the sun. But it wasn't the shimmer that caught her attention. In the background, out of focus and easy to miss, was an old windmill, the kind with rusted galvanized steel blades atop a weathered wood tower. At the base of the windmill was a redwood sign, too blurry and distant to read. But she would recognize it if she saw it in person. The picture was dated May 11 of last year. Below the picture were the words CAMPING IN MY FAVORITE SPOT IN ALEXANDRIA. A GOOD DAY'S FIND.

God knows. Tracy's words echoed in the night air. Words that applied to Niesha as much as they did to Matt and Jana.

If they were meant to find her, they would.

"Girls, girls, come in, come in. Look at you." Lucille, her snowy white bob reflecting a pink glow from her flowing fuchsia caftan, kept her fingertips on a narrow glass table in her foyer as she stepped back. "Let me guess." She pointed at Tracy. "You have your mother's eyes, and I'm guessing you're the oldest. Tracy, right?"

Tracy nodded, the same look of surprise on her face Amy was sure she was showing. Had they met her years ago and just didn't remember? Lucille turned to her next. "You must be Amy. So pretty. You're the teacher, I think. And Robin. How are your parents, dear?"

"F-fine."

"Now introduce me to this lovely lady." She held her hand out, palm up, toward Jana.

Jana had not wanted to leave Amy's side all morning and was thrilled to join the grown-ups on a girls' getaway. When Matt was invited to go to the toy museum with a friend from their play group, Robin declared it was a sign that their day would be filled with serendipitous encounters. If this greeting was any indication, they were off to a good start.

"This is Jana," Amy said.

"I am honored to meet you, sweet girl. Let's go sit in the living room. Pardon the boxes. I've lived here fifty-three years and accumulated much." She led them into a room as colorful and surprising as she was. Amy had expected to see classic furnishings, similar to Columbia's. Instead, she felt as though she were walking into the Taj Mahal. From the navy and indigo area rug to the scarlet, purple, and gold wall hanging, the ambiance felt like stepping into another world. Intricately carved wood tables were arranged next to chairs and a love seat upholstered in block-printed fabrics and accessorized with fringed pillows and bolsters adorned with little gold bells. Amy half expected to hear sitar music in the background.

"This is..." She fought for a word that would do the room justice.

"Gorgeous," Tracy whispered.

They sat on armchairs with deep cushions. In the center of the room, a white china tea service and bottles of orange juice rested on a glass-topped wicker table shaped like an elephant with a raised trunk. "Do you like chai?" Lucille asked. When all of her adult guests nodded enthusiastically, Lucille poured tea, then handed Jana a bottle of juice followed by a plate of cookies. Amy had to look away from Jana, afraid she would laugh at the expression of complete awe on her round face.

"You've done some traveling in your life, haven't you, Lucille?" Robin, far more of an expert on the origin—and cost—of the room's decor, looked around with as much wonder in her eyes as that of the six-year-old in the chair across from her.

"Oh my, yes. My husband was a homebody. I was fifty-seven when he passed, and after moping around for a year as if it were *my* life that had ended, I decided it was high time I started really living. So I spent the next twenty-five years doing everything I always wanted to do. I saw a lot, bought a lot, and gave a lot." Her eyes crinkled over the rim of a china cup embellished with a gold and teal geometric pattern. "But enough about me. You came to talk about my sister and your grandmother." She set her cup on the saucer in her lap. "What can I tell you?"

Amy glanced at Robin, who turned to Tracy. Why hadn't they scripted this, or at least decided who would talk first? Might as well jump in. "How long did Elizabeth and Grandma Pearl know each other?"

"Oh, goodness, most of their lives. They were besties, as they say now, even after Elizabeth went to college and then moved to Washington, DC during the war." She pressed a pink-nailed finger to her lips. "She was a code girl," she whispered.

"Really?" Amy's response merged with "Seriously?" and "She was?" from Tracy and Robin.

"Yes indeed. She wouldn't talk about it for many years. They weren't just sworn to secrecy, they were told they would be *shot* if they didn't keep their mouths shut." Lucille clutched the front of her caftan. "Elizabeth was a language student at St. Mary's in Indiana. French, German, and Italian. That's why she was recruited. In her later years, she shared some things with me. Can you imagine having a part in breaking a code that allowed our submarines to sink German U-boats before they had a chance to attack our ships? She had so many stories like that. And after the war..." Lucille's voice lowered, as if she were afraid her living room was bugged. "Elizabeth worked for the CIG."

"You mean the CIA?" Tracy asked.

"Well, yes, but it was the Central Intelligence Group first." Lucille pressed her palms together. "My big sister was a spy!"

Amy didn't dare make eye contact with Tracy or Robin. Was this for real, or had the years turned Elizabeth into a legend in Lucille's eyes?

Tracy cleared her throat. "Elizabeth came to visit Grandma Pearl every year, didn't she?"

"Oh yes. At least once a year. Sometimes every month, until... Well, you know, Elizabeth wasn't much of a traveler in her later years." She blinked, and her lips curved in a strained smile. "Pearl was always so kind to Elizabeth. My sister wasn't...well, I guess nowadays we'd say she didn't always have a filter." Lucille grinned. "If something popped into her head, it generally popped out of her mouth. Yet Pearl always welcomed her."

Robin nodded and smiled, but Amy recognized it as her impatient smile. "We found a newspaper clipping from 1987. Elizabeth was the one who reported the theft of a painting from our grandmother's house. Do you know anything about that?"

Lucille set her cup on the glass-topped table. "More tea, anyone?"

Amy wished she'd brought Matt the supersleuth with his lie-detecting theories. Was Lucille stalling? It certainly looked like she was. The three women all declined more tea. Amy's had just cooled enough to be drinkable. They waited in silence while Lucille topped off her cup. The woman must have deadened the heat receptors in her mouth from years of hot chai.

"I do remember hearing about the theft," she said. "Elizabeth was visiting Pearl when it happened. She came home early from the trip, quite distraught. She thought the reporter took it."

Amy glanced at Tracy. The alarm on her face hinted that she was thinking the same thing. Columbia? Had Grandma Pearl really suspected her? That would explain her cold reception to Columbia's prying questions.

"Reporter?" Tracy asked. "From the Canton paper?"

"No." Lucille stared at the far wall, where a flowing batik fabric was draped in deep waves across several metal pegs. Amy could easily imagine it covering the place where Green Girl had hung. "A reporter from St. Louis. Elizabeth knew the artist and wanted to promote his work, but right after the reporter interviewed Pearl, the painting was stolen."

The room seemed suddenly charged with electricity. Amy set her cup on the small table next to her and folded her hands on her lap. "Do you remember the name of the artist?"

Once again, Lucille's gaze fastened on the swath of fabric. "Oh, goodness. That was a very long time ago."

"We think his initials are JW," Robin said.

"Well now." Lucille rubbed the crease above her nose with one finger. "This old brain isn't what it once was." She took a quick breath and flashed a dazzling smile. "I have several boxes of Elizabeth's old letters and papers I need to sort through. If I find anything helpful, I will most certainly let you know. I'm sure you'd like to find out what happened to that beautiful painting."

Tracy's eyebrow rose. "You're familiar with it?"

"Well, yes, of course. I visited Pearl several times with Elizabeth. The last time was six years ago, just a few months before Elizabeth passed. They hadn't seen each other since…a very long time. I think they both knew it would be the last time they saw one another. It was sad, but I believe they each had the opportunity to say what needed to be said. Forgiveness for past hurts and a few confessions." Her eyes grew misty.

Confessions? About what? Amy tried to formulate a way to ask, but Robin beat her to it.

"That had to have been very emotional to witness, Lucille. I'm glad to hear they had the chance to forgive each other." She took a sip of tea, then cleared her throat. "Did they talk about the painting? I would hate to think either of them was left with any hard feelings about it."

Lucille pressed her lips together. "I believe they did. I remember Elizabeth saying, 'It's been more than thirty years. Have you finally been able to forgive me?' Pearl patted her hand and said, 'I did that long ago.'"

Amy swallowed hard. Should she ask? If she came right out and said, "Did Elizabeth steal the painting?" would that offend Lucille, or would it give her a chance to finally share what she'd been keeping a secret for years? Maybe something not quite so direct. "Do you know, specifically, what Elizabeth was referring to?"

Lucille's hand fluttered to her mouth. "Well, I—I think that was something just between the two of them, don't you?" Setting down her cup and saucer again, she stood, abruptly but gracefully. "I think we might be boring this young lady. Let me show you Elizabeth's room." She kept her gaze on Jana. "There are a couple of pictures of your great-grandmother you might like to see." With that, she turned and walked down a hallway.

After exchanging looks, the others followed. The focal point of the room papered in a green and white floral pattern was a four-poster bed with a lace canopy and a vintage candlewick bedspread. Raised French knots on the white spread outlined the shape of a handled basket overflowing with flowers. But it was the small decorative pillow sitting on the doily-covered nightstand that drew Amy's attention. She stepped around the foot of the bed for a closer look.

Lucille gave a light laugh. "That little pillow is very old. Elizabeth always used it as a pincushion. She joked that it was her voodoo pillow. Of course, neither of us believed in such things."

The lace-trimmed pillow showed signs of age and wear. There were bald patches on the velvet. *Dark green* velvet.

And, if she wasn't mistaken, the yellowed lace was the exact same pattern as the trim on the dress in the picture now displayed, once again, above Grandma Pearl's fireplace.

November 14, 1937

My dear, faithful paper friend. If you were a real person, I'm sure by now you would be quite exasperated with me, for I only write about John these days. And I must watch myself carefully or Richard will think John is more important to me than he is. Thankfully, the two are becoming fast friends, so we often talk about John's adventures together. His stories are such a welcome reprieve from daily life in little ol' Canton that seems so terribly mundane now. All I once wrote about—hair and fashion and movie stars and who likes who—cannot hold a candle to all of the wonders I can envision when John talks of his travels. He is truly the most exciting thing in this boring town.

John and I took another walk around the block after church today. Mother has spent enough time with him that she no longer thinks he is the Big Bad Wolf. I believe everyone else is used to it now, so they don't stare anymore. All but one person anyway. Bess is mad at me again. She really likes John as more than a friend even though I tell her that is silly and wrong. We invited her to walk with us this morning, but her mother wasn't feeling well so she had to go home. She is mad because I chose to go without her. "It's not fair!" she yelled when she left. "You already have a boyfriend! You can't have both of them!"

Sometimes I wonder why we are friends. True, we do have a lot of laughs together, but we are so very, very different in almost every way. I wish she didn't always think we are in competition. It's that way with everything—who has the best grades, the longest hair, the most boys paying attention to her. I don't want to compete with anyone for anything except maybe in tennis.

Speaking of Bess's mom, I think I forgot to write some big news. She is going to have a baby! It's so strange to think of Bess having a little brother or sister when she is actually old enough to be a mother herself. Bess isn't happy about it because she thinks she will be stuck home watching the baby while the rest of us are out having fun. She is probably right, but I can't wait to hold a newborn. Maybe I will be the one staying home to watch the little one while she goes to parties and dances!

Anyway, back to John. He is so sad. Gänse's sail date got put off indefinitely, and he doesn't know why. I certainly made things worse today by talking about an article I read about the ongoing search for Amelia Earhart's plane, and then I said something so stupid about how that, along with the crash of the Hindenburg and everything happening in Europe, made me hope 1938 would be a better year. John stopped walking, and when he looked at me, I thought he would break down crying. "There is little hope for a better future for so many of my friends back home," he said. I felt so awful! I apologized for being so naive and tried to change the subject. I asked what he is painting now. He said he didn't feel like painting, because he had thought that by now Gänse would be his subject. Being my usual impulsive self, I asked to see his paintings. I was hoping he would invite me to his house because I think maybe his studio is behind the secret door, but instead he said he had one he could give me. It used to hang in his uncle's gallery, but they were making room for new pieces, so he had one in his car. It is a picture of a beautiful castle. I told him I could not take it, but he said it just made him sad to look at it because he feared he might not ever see it again. I hung it above my dresser. It will remind me to pray for Gänse every day.

Good night, dear diary.

Chapter Sixteen

Ordering off the "build your own" menu at Stacked became a hysterical competition between Amy, Tracy, and Robin. With choices like goat cheese, chipotle aioli, fried jalapeños, white bean hummus, bacon maple jam, and pickled red onions, all three ended up with giant, deliciously messy burgers. Jana was content with her chicken strips. Between mopping up drips, they mulled over their visit with Lucille.

"What did you guys think about Elizabeth's 'voodoo' pillow?" Tracy wiggled fingers coated in barbecue sauce and made a face that was supposed to be scary but came off as hilarious.

Robin handed her another napkin from the pile in the middle of the table. "Seems to me, Elizabeth might have had some serious anger issues."

"Or maybe guilt issues," Amy added. "If she stole the painting and harbored that secret for decades..."

"But maybe the painting was supposed to be hers all along," Tracy suggested. "If the pillow was really made from the same dress, isn't it likely it was her dress, that she is our Green Girl?"

"Good point." The thought had crossed Amy's mind, but she had dismissed it because any explanation for Grandma Pearl having the painting and Elizabeth having a piece of the dress made

Grandma look bad. Not to mention that her feelings about the painting would alter drastically if the young woman in the velvet dress was actually Elizabeth.

"Of course, we have no way of knowing if the velvet came from the same dress," Tracy said.

"The lace was the same pattern," Amy said. "I'm sure of it."

Robin took a slurp of strawberry shake. "So Elizabeth was a code girl and a spy. Maybe, anyway. What did Grandma Pearl do during the war?"

"She fell in love," Tracy said with a wink.

Amy searched her mental files for anything Grandma had said about working during the war. So many women did. "Something else to research."

"I'll ask Mom about it," Robin said. "Grandma would have turned twenty just a couple of weeks after Pearl Harbor. Maybe she was a Rosie the Riveter. There were women from all over Missouri working in the aviation industry."

Tracy swirled a french fry in a combination of ketchup and ranch dressing. "Interesting that we keep coming back to the World War II era. Both professors had books on the Nazis confiscating art, the payment for Green Girl was made in 1937, the castle painting was done in 1935, and now Lucille brings up Elizabeth working as a code breaker during the war."

Amy pushed aside half of her burger and fries, ready to move on to the next phase of their adventure. "Hopefully, we'll get some of our other questions answered in a few minutes." They'd rearranged their plan for the day and decided on an early lunch, leaving as much of the afternoon open for the gallery as needed, and agreeing that the surplus store was optional, depending on time. "Let's decide ahead who's going to ask what."

"I say we look for the oldest person working there," Tracy said. "More chance of them knowing something about the way they did things in the thirties, or where they keep old records, *if* they do."

"And Robin's our art expert," Amy added, "so our first step is scoping out the gallery for old people Robin can talk to."

Robin laughed. "That'll fly. Hi, you look really old, can I talk to you?"

To Amy's surprise, their first conversation with a staff member actually started much the way Robin had facetiously proposed. The dapper bespectacled man in the three-piece suit sitting behind the desk directly in front of the entrance appeared to be at least as old as Professor Maura Childs. "Welcome to Wolfram & Randulph Fine Arts, ladies. How may I be of service?"

Robin stepped up to the desk. "We're looking for information on a painting that was either bought or commissioned by Wolfram and Randulph in 1937. Do you keep records going back that far?"

"Ma'am, you're talking to the right person. My name is Hyrum Fischer. My father was the registrar when the gallery opened in 1928, and I took over his position in 1963. Since I retired fourteen years ago, I am now a volunteer archivist."

Robin handed him a color picture of Green Girl. "We're hoping to find out who the young woman is, and maybe something about the artist."

He took the photograph. "Stunning. Tell me what you know about it."

Tracy and Amy, who was holding Jana's hand, drew closer to the desk. Tracy pulled the record of payment they'd found in Grandma's attic out of her purse. She'd put it in a sealed bag and kept it pressed flat in a spiral notebook. "This is all we have to go on."

Hyrum's bushy brows danced as he examined it. "*A Study in Emerald Velvet.* A little slice of our history right here in my hand." He set it down and opened the silver laptop in front of him.

His fingers flew across the keys. So much for the stereotypes about older adults and technology. After several minutes he shook his head. "I'm sorry. There's nothing in our database. Can you tell me anything else about it? Is P. Wallace the artist?"

"No. We think the artist's initials may be JW."

The unruly white eyebrows shot above the frames of his glasses. "Well...I have a possible educated guess. Johannes Wolfram was the nephew of Otto Wolfram, the gallery's founder. Quite an accomplished artist in his younger years."

"Would he have been painting back in the thirties?"

"Most definitely. We have several of his works on display. Would you like to see them?"

"Absolutely," Robin answered.

Hyrum looked beyond them, as if viewing a scene from the past. "Johannes died in 1999. He was a fascinating man. He and his wife were generous philanthropists for the arts. He had much to do with developing the art department at Culver-Stockton College."

Amy glanced at Robin and Tracy, and they shared a silent sense of discovery.

"I visited their house in Canton many, many years ago." Ridges formed above his eyebrows. "There was something…"

As his thoughts seemed to drift back in time, the women waited. Finally, Amy prodded with, "Would you happen to have the address? We live in Canton."

He blinked several times until his focus was back on them, but the look of confusion remained. "I don't know if I have the address, but I drove up there a few years back and found it. When they arrived in St. Louis, Johannes and his father, Fritz, worked here, as partners. But something changed, philosophical differences between Fritz and his brother Otto, I believe. There was always an undercurrent of tension between the two of them. My father spoke about them being 'unequally yoked.' Father had a great deal of respect for Fritz. I think he feared Otto. Anyway, when Fritz was offered a teaching position at Culver-Stockton, they moved. Their relationship fell apart after the war."

Hyrum lowered his glasses and rubbed the bridge of his nose. "They had a two-story redbrick house with lots of fancy white gingerbread trim. On a corner, about a block from the college. I was probably only about ten when we visited, but I have vivid memories of being astonished, and a bit frightened, though I can't to this day remember why. The interior was absolutely palatial. Marble floors, crystal chandeliers. The family came from Germany in the 1930s, escaping the Nazis. There was always an air of mystery about them. Secrets of some sort. Who knows what they saw or were involved with before coming to America?" He tapped his chin and the furrows on his forehead deepened. "They had a statue in the front yard. A woman in a flowing gown with a bird perched on her hand. It disappeared sometime in the nineties."

"Disappeared?" Robin whispered.

"I remember it," Tracy said, lowering her voice on the last word as if suddenly realizing where she was. "I know where the house is."

"Good. I don't know if it's still in the family. If you find out anything about the disappearance of the statue, please let me know. It's just one more piece of the Wolfram family puzzle."

Amy felt a slight chill at the mention of puzzle pieces. It was the same metaphor she'd used since finding Green Girl.

"Otto was a true enigma," Hyrum said. "Nicest man to his customers, but no one dared cross him. He dressed like a character right out of a gangster movie. Pinstriped suits, wingtip shoes. A very tight-lipped man. 'A closed book,' my father used to say. The staff had to exit the building by six o'clock sharp every night. Otto said he wanted his people to have dinner with their families, but there were rumors about packages arriving at the back door after hours. No one knew what was in them. If you wanted to keep your job, you knew better than to ask." He pushed back his chair and stood slowly, grabbing a shiny black cane with a carved silver knob to steady himself. He handed the plastic bag back to Tracy. "Do you know who P. Wallace was?"

A grin spread across Tracy's face. "Pearl Wallace was our grandmother."

"Pearl? Really?" He looked like a child on Christmas morning.

"Does the name mean something to you?" Amy asked.

"Well, I think...I just might have a little surprise for you." He motioned for them to follow him and continued talking as they did. "I imagine you want to keep your painting, but if you are ever interested in selling, or even loaning, I believe the gallery would pay a pretty penny...if we can prove it's a Wolfram original." His words picked up speed with every step. As he walked, he pulled his sleeve back and checked his watch. "Our manager had a lunch meeting but should be back soon. I'll introduce you. He might be able to answer more of your questions than I can. For now"—he gestured to the arched entrance of a large white-walled room displaying framed art—"let's have a look at a few other Wolframs."

The first two paintings were small landscapes. In the foreground of the first, a woman's straw hat with trailing ribbons hung from a tree branch. In the background, the forest was partially shrouded by fog. In the next, heavy mist rose from a calm stream, nearly engulfing an arched footbridge. A wicker picnic basket sat on the bridge, a blue-and-white-checked cloth peeking out from beneath the cover. A small plate holding a slice of cake with a lit candle in it sat beside the basket. There was something ethereal about both paintings. Robin stepped within inches of one of them and said the brushstrokes were similar to the two paintings they had.

"You have more than one?" Hyrum peered over the top of his glasses.

Amy told him about the painting of Neuschwanstein Castle. "It said 1935 on the back."

He gave a thoughtful nod. "Do you know what Neuschwanstein Castle was used for at the end of the war?"

"We've read about the confiscated art stored there by the Nazis."

"A travesty. I remember tears in Fritz's eyes as he described works of art that were stolen from museums and galleries, and even homes. He and Johannes knew many artists who died in concentration camps or who managed to flee but were never heard from again. Johannes worked here part-time as a bookkeeper. One day, a year or so after the end of the war, Fritz came in waving a telegram and yelling at Otto. He read it out loud. A good friend, a renowned Jewish artist, and his wife and daughter had died at Ravensbrück. Johannes crumpled to the floor and sobbed in a way I have never since heard a man cry." Hyrum's voice quavered at the memory. He ran a hand under his glasses. "I was only seven or eight at the time, but I remember thinking it strange that Fritz's anger over something that happened in Germany seemed directed at Otto."

Jana's hand tightened in Amy's. She smiled reassuringly at Jana's worried look. The sudden sobering in the mood had clearly affected her. "It's okay, sweetie," she whispered.

"But now…" Hyrum waved in a dismissive gesture, as if pushing the past behind him. "For the rest of the tour." He tapped his cane twice on the floor, renewed excitement in his eyes. Amy got the impression he'd shown them the landscapes just to build the anticipation for whatever was going to come next. "In my opinion," Hyrum said as they walked around a dividing wall, "this next one is the finest Wolfram in our collection. There is always a sense of intrigue in his paintings. They make one want to know more." He gestured to a painting the same size as Green Girl. "I have long had a question about this one. I have wondered why all of the words in the title are not capitalized. I thought possibly the engraver had made a mistake." He grinned, eyes twinkling. "I believe you ladies have supplied the answer to my question."

In the painting, shafts of colored light fell on delicate hands folded on an open Bible. A chorus of quiet gasps filled the high-ceilinged room as Robin held her right hand up to the painting. Her pearl ring was an exact match to the one on the woman's hand. On the bottom edge of the frame was a brass plaque engraved with the words, *A Pearl of great price.*

Chapter Seventeen

Cameron James, the gallery manager, reminded Amy of a stereotypical car salesman more than an art gallery manager. She couldn't put her finger on it, but the way he almost bowed as he pumped each of their hands in turn made her feel uncomfortable.

"Mr. James," Robin said as they stood in front of the picture of hands folded on a Bible, "before we start peppering you with questions about Johannes Wolfram, there's something else you might be able to help us with. Did Emmett Mullens, a security guard with Overland Protective Services, ever work for you?"

Not surprisingly, the question seemed to confuse him for a moment. "Yes. Recently. May I ask why you want to know?"

Amy watched Robin, wondering how she would answer. Robin didn't miss a beat. "We're trying to find his girlfriend. She's an art student at Culver-Stockton, and we love her work."

A slow smile spread across his face. "Niesha Carter?"

"Yes."

"I actually have one of her pieces on display. Gutsy girl. She just walked in one day with her portfolio and asked me to look at her work. So much talent. I assume we'll have a whole wall dedicated to her someday."

"Have you had any contact with her in the past week?"

"No. She hasn't been in since Emmett left."

Amy watched his face for any sign of his opinion of Emmett. "Did he leave on good terms?"

"Yes. He took on a private job. In Canton, I believe. I assumed he wanted to be closer to Niesha."

Trying to hide her reaction to that statement wasn't easy. When Robin thanked the man for the information, Amy could tell she was restraining her emotions too.

"This way." Mr. James motioned for them to follow. "Johannes Wolfram could have had a very successful career as an artist, but he gave it all up sometime in the forties. Unfortunately, I don't know the details. A personal tragedy, I'm told." He pointed at the painting Amy now assumed was Grandma Pearl's hands folded on a Bible and shook his head. "Our records show this was done in 1941. It could well have been one of his last works. "Whatever the reason, his decision to stop painting was a tragedy for all of us who came after him."

Came after him? "Are you related to Johannes?" Amy asked.

"In a roundabout way." Did his smile seem to flatten a bit? "My great-grandmother was Otto Wolfram's second wife. Together they had two children. My grandmother was one of them." A corner of his mouth rose upward, as if he was trying to make it take the shape of a smile, but something had clearly altered the car salesman persona. He swept a hand toward the painting. "This, like the rest of Johannes's work, was crated in our back room when I came to work here. It was a while before I found out why. There'd been a fissure in the family.

"But a few years back, after my great-grandmother died, my grandmother finally began sharing what she remembered. She had so many stories about Otto, and a few about Johannes. He joined the army and became part of the MFAA, the Monuments, Fine Art, and Archives program, which came out of Roosevelt's American Commission for the Protection and Salvage of Artistic and Historic Monuments in War Areas, more commonly known as the Roberts Commission, after its chair, Supreme Court Justice Owen J. Roberts. Johannes's art history knowledge, as well as his familiarity with Germany and the German language, made him a perfect candidate." His chin rose, giving Amy the sense that he was anticipating some form of adoration for his fact retention. "Have you seen the movie *The Monuments Men*?"

Amy exchanged glances with Robin and Tracy, and all three nodded.

"Johannes was one of them. He was part of the small group of American troops that entered Neuschwanstein Castle on May 4, 1945, along with James Rorimer, the future director of the Metropolitan Museum of Art. My grandmother said he described the castle as being in complete chaos, with art treasures stashed and scattered everywhere. Apparently, the Nazis started clearing out the castle before their arrival, because some of the rooms were empty. Some of the lower floors had been recently plastered and paintings from France hung on the wall. They found tapestries, rare engravings, drawings, furniture, and entire libraries of Paris collectors filling the rooms." His eyes widened as he described the bounty, then he abruptly held up both hands. "My apologies. This is a particular passion for me. I could go on for hours."

"No apology needed," Robin said. "It's all fascinating."

"Let me show you the other Wolfram works. We only have three more. My grandmother said there were others, but we have no idea where they are. So, you can see what remarkable treasures you have. Hyrum mentioned he told you we would gladly pay a premium if you should ever decide to sell or loan. That is absolutely true." He ushered them to a wall at the back of the gallery. The card mounted at the top of the wall said, JOHANNES WOLFRAM, 1918–1999.

Amy studied the paintings. One depicted a blanket spread on the grass with the iconic silver dome of Culver-Stockton's Henderson Hall in the background. An envelope and an opened letter lay on the blanket. In the second painting, a man sat on one side of a park bench, wearing a brimmed hat, head bowed. His hand rested on the empty half of the bench, palm up, as if waiting for someone to slip her hand in his.

The third canvas was the one that evoked the strongest emotion in Amy. A table set for two. A single dripping candle had burned almost down to its silver candleholder. On one plate rested a half-eaten crust of bread and a partially peeled orange. A cloth napkin was crumpled beside it. The other napkin was folded neatly. And the other plate was empty. "It's like, in all of these, except for *A Pearl of great price*, he's searching for or waiting for someone."

Hyrum, who'd been so quiet Amy had forgotten about him, stepped closer and quietly said, "What if the one he was waiting for was your grandmother?"

Five sleuths gathered around Amy's kitchen table late Monday afternoon. Tracy and Robin had come in to sort bags from the surplus store, but curiosity had kept them there long after each said they needed to get home to make supper. They sat with pens, paper, Amy's laptop, and three cell phones, searching for any information they could find on Johannes Wolfram. To everyone's surprise, no one's more than his mother's, Kai showed an interest in their mystery. He and Matt were looking through Matt's lie-detecting book. Jana joined them at the table, busy making a camping list that included five of her lovies by name.

Robin raised her hands in exasperation. "If we were looking for someone alive today, I'd say it was a cover-up. Johannes shows up in Otto Wolfram's obituary, but nowhere else. And I couldn't even find his obituary, or Fritz's."

"Wait." Amy enlarged a picture on her screen. "Here's a newspaper article about the ten-year anniversary of the gallery. There he is!" She read the caption as the others jumped out of their seats and huddled around her. "'Celebrating ten years of offering high-quality art to St. Louis are, from left to right, Otto, Johannes, and Fritz Wolfram.'"

The man in the middle was taller and younger than the other two. Though the black-and-white picture was dark and grainy, it was clear this younger version of the man in the scarecrow costume was extremely handsome.

"What are the chances Hyrum was right?" Amy asked. "What if there was something between Grandma and Johannes? He painted *Pearl of great price* in 1941. She would have married Grandpa four years after that, giving Johannes lots of time to be pining for her."

"Could be," Robin said. "He was wearing a wedding ring in that picture of him with Grandma, so clearly he got over her at some point."

Amy pressed her hand to her chest and gave an exaggerated sigh. "But he never loved his wife the way he loved his Pearl of great price."

Robin laughed. "Why, again, did you decide not to become a playwright?"

Kai rolled his eyes and shook his head.

Amy recognized a teachable moment when she saw one. "Did you boys know the title of that painting is a Bible reference?" She looked up the passage on her phone, then got up and grabbed her Bible from the top of a pile of books and notebooks on the built-in hutch. Another teaching point—not all knowledge came from a Google search. She laid the Bible open and began to read. "'Again, the kingdom of heaven is like a merchant looking for fine pearls. When he found one of great value, he went away and sold everything he had and bought it.'"

Robin turned to her son. "What do you think that means?"

Kai shrugged. "I guess that nothing is worth more than knowing Jesus, right?"

"Good answer." Robin held her hand out for a fist bump.

Kai's eye roll gave a curtain call, but he complied, then squinted at the ring on his mother's hand as if seeing it for the first time. "What's this thing worth, anyway?" He gave his mother a zany grin that somehow translated into dollar signs in his eyes.

Laughing, Robin snatched her hand away. "We need to dig around in the attic and see if we can find Grandma's diaries. Mom said she found them when she was a teenager, and Grandma made her promise not to tell any of her secrets. Maybe she was talking about her first love and didn't want Grandpa to hear about it."

"Why would she keep her diaries if they were full of secrets?" Kai asked. "I don't get why girls write all that stuff down anyway."

Tracy smiled. "If she kept them until Aunt Ruth was in her teens, there's a good chance they're still around. That's our next attic mission. After our finding Niesha trip."

Amy rubbed her eyes and closed her laptop. "I say we take a break and talk camping." She nodded toward the three bags from their trip to the surplus store.

"Finally!" Matt jumped up. He pulled out two sleeping bags, a lantern, a set of six hot dog forks, and two pie irons. "What are these?"

"They are magic," Robin said. "You put a dollop of pie filling between two pieces of bread and toast it over the fire and voilà! You have a pudgy pie."

"You can even make grilled cheese and Reuben pudgy pies," Tracy added.

Amy smiled as a memory surfaced. "Remember when we made that sandwich for Dad with raisin bread, cream cheese, pickles, strawberry jam, and Fritos?"

"And jalapeños," Tracy reminded her. "He ate the whole thing and asked for another one."

"Cool." Matt's eyes danced. Amy was certain her dad would have loved this boy. "Can I go get the camping box from the storage closet?"

Amy nodded, and he ran toward the spare room that would one day become a guest room doubling as her office.

"What do we still need?" Robin asked. "For once, I'm grateful I'm married to a saver. We haven't camped since Kai was six, but we've still got all our equipment."

"Same." Tracy picked up her phone. "I took inventory and made a list. Pretty much all we need is food and clothes." She handed her phone to Amy.

The list took up three pages. Amy skimmed it, finding a few things she hadn't thought of. Duct tape, cutting board, binoculars, bandannas. Some of those could be borrowed from her more equipped sleuthing partners. "I think we're doing okay. I still have my tent, camp stove, water filter, sleeping bag and pad, even a pair of zip-off shorts that are hopelessly out of fashion, but I'm still bringing them."

"I've got my headphones and iPad," Kai said, eyes shimmering with mischief. "Me and my friends have a whole schedule figured out for games." He looked from his mom to his aunts, his teen grin clearly saying he knew how much they abhorred bad grammar. "I got PlayerUnknown's Battleground, Fortnite, League of Nations. I'm just hoping I have a good enough signal the whole week so we—" Under the glare of three pairs of eyes, he broke character and laughed.

Tracy stood and stretched. "Now I really need to get home and start supper. I'll ask Jeff about Fritz Wolfram. Even though we couldn't find anything, I'm sure he has access to college archives. And I'm going to drive past that house and get the address before I talk to my editor about the disappearing statue."

Robin stood and picked up her purse. "We better head home too. I'll call Grace and see what we can dig up at the library. Amy, what's your assignment?"

"Getting the three of us packed has to be my top priority. If I have any free time, I want to focus on narrowing our search area for

Niesha. I'll call Lisa and see if she's heard anything else that will give us a clue where to start looking tomorrow."

After hugs, Tracy, Robin, and Kai left. Matt barreled through the living room carrying a box marked *Camping Stuff*. But instead of tearing into it, he set it on the table. "Mom?" His tone was wary. "Niesha ran away because she was scared, right?"

"We think so." Where was this going?

"Blake told me about a kid from his old foster home who ran away because he didn't want to move again."

Lord, I need wisdom. "What happened?"

"He got caught and he had to move to another foster home anyway."

"Matt?" She patted the kitchen chair Robin had just vacated. "What are you thinking?"

He took an apple from the bowl in the center of the table. "Nothing. I just…" His chest shuddered. "What if Mama wants Jana but not me?"

The molecules in the air around them seemed to freeze in place. He had voiced the words Amy had tried to shut out of her mind.

Jana set her pencil down, and she shook her head. "I won't go without you. We are going to get adoptized and everything is going to be okay."

"But what if—"

"Shh." Amy put one arm around Matt and the other around Jana and hugged her children close. "God knows. He has it all worked out." She spoke to herself as much as to them. And then a bit of wisdom from Corrie ten Boom floated up from the past. "'Never be afraid to trust an unknown future to a known God.'"

November 20, 1937

Mama finished the birthday dresses for Bess and me. I absolutely love them! We've had "twin" dresses since we were eight and found out we were born two days apart. I suppose this will be the last year. It is kind of a childish thing. We are going to wear them for Thanksgiving and for all the Christmas parties.

I got a letter from Gänse yesterday! She is so witty and clever, and we have read many of the same books. She said the strangest thing: "I am trying to memorize long passages in case the day comes that we can no longer have Papa's library." I assume she means they will not be able to pack all of their books when they come to America. Anyway, I do think we are going to be the best of friends. That will likely cause a problem with Bess, but I'm not going to worry about that.

Gänse thanked me for being John's friend and asked me to please try to make him think of happy things. That made me want to cry. I can only imagine how sad his letters must make her. This is like Romeo and Juliet, only it is an evil man and not their families keeping them apart. Please, God, let their story have a happy ending.

Good night, dear diary.

Chapter Eighteen

When her phone rang around nine thirty on Tuesday morning, Amy breathed a sigh of gratitude. She'd left a message for Lisa half an hour earlier. Hands greasy from making hamburger patties, she tapped the speaker icon with one finger and thanked Lisa for getting back to her.

"Could we meet again? At the grocery store maybe?"

The young woman's tone made Amy's shoulders tighten. "Is Niesha okay?"

"I don't know. I don't want to talk about it on the phone."

"Of course. I'm leaving town right after noon. Are you free this morning?" She glanced at the clock, then at Jana finishing her second bowl of cereal and Matt adding yet a few more "essentials" to his backpack. Surprisingly, they were just about packed and ready with almost three hours to go.

"Yes. Is twenty minutes too soon?" Lisa sounded breathless, as if she'd been running. "I have something to show you."

"We'll make that work. I'll meet you by the ice cream toppings again."

She hung up, then turned at Matt's "Whoa." Aluminum water bottle dangling from one finger, he gaped at her. "That sounded like real spy stuff."

"It just might be." Amy sighed.

Jana set her spoon down. "Is somebody going to hurt Niesha?" Her big brown eyes gazed up at Amy.

Had it been a mistake to include the kids in their search? What had started out as simply an intriguing mystery might now be something involving real danger, at least for the young woman they prayed for every night. "I hope not, honey." She forced a bright smile. "What other treats do we need to pick up at the store? We have to get pie filling for our pudgy pies. My favorite is blueberry, probably because that was Grandma Pearl's favorite, but I bet you two would love cherry. Or chocolate! Maybe with marshmallows? They melt and get all gooey." She was babbling, but it seemed to be helping. "Let's go buy some. How fast can you get dressed?"

As they ran upstairs, she took a moment to update Tracy and Robin.

With Matt leading the charge, they were out the door in less than ten minutes and waiting by the hot fudge five minutes early. Lisa approached them wearing a lightweight pink sweatshirt with the hood up. Not a fashion statement, Amy knew. The strap of a large messenger bag crossed her chest. She had dark circles under her eyes, and her face looked pale.

Lisa pulled what looked like a piece of cardstock out of her bag. "Niesha and I met in the art club three years ago. We volunteered to plan photo treasure hunts. They turned out to be so much fun, we kept doing them, just the two of us. We always put the first clue in a mailbox that's part of a mixed media display she made for the gallery on campus. The last time I saw her, she told me to keep checking the mailbox. That's where she left the message I said smelled smoky. This morning I found this." She handed the paper to Amy. "Look closely."

Amy recognized the statue immediately. The figure of a Union soldier in full dress uniform stood atop a large white obelisk. "The Unknown Soldiers monument up in Keokuk." Only about half an hour away, the Keokuk National Cemetery was just over the Missouri-Iowa border. She studied the pencil drawing. The detail was astonishing. Niesha had even captured the texture of the granite. Below the carved inscription, *In Memory of the Unknown Dead*, was a laurel wreath in raised relief. Amy pulled the paper closer. Penciled in to look like an inscription that followed the curve of the bottom of the wreath were several numbers followed by a single letter: 7-19 4P. Amy looked up at Lisa. "Today's the nineteenth. Is she asking you to meet her there at four o'clock today?"

"I think so. But"—Lisa glanced behind her—"I saw Emmett last night, leaning on a car across the street from my apartment. I think he's watching me. I called the police, but he was gone by the time they got there."

"Oh, honey." Instinctively, Amy put a reassuring hand on Lisa's arm. "Do you have a friend you can stay with?"

"Yeah. I'm gonna stay on campus with my old roommate. I don't think Emmett would hurt me. He just wants to find out where Niesha is. But that's why I can't meet her." Pleading eyes asked a question Amy heard loud and clear.

"Do you believe God orchestrates our steps, Lisa?"

"Y-yes."

"Well, my family and I are going camping this afternoon, mostly to look for Niesha. We're staying in Alexandria tonight. That's about ten minutes from this very spot. I'll go meet her."

Lisa's wide eyes filled with disbelief. "Tell her you're Angel."

Amy gave her the most reassuring smile she could muster. "I'll do that."

Lisa's eyes reddened. "You d-don't even know her. Wh-why?" A sob ripped from her throat, and she threw her arms around Amy. "Thank you. Thank you. I didn't think God was listening to me, but He sent you!"

"Amy!" Tracy sprinted across the Country Market parking lot toward her. "I want to hear everything you learned from Lisa, but first"—she paused to catch her breath—"are you caught up enough to come with me to meet Jeff at the Fountain? He has a break in five minutes."

"Sure." Amy pushed the remote to open her car doors. "Is this about Fritz?"

"Fritz and then some." Tracy pointed to the bag Matt carried. "Anything perishable?"

Matt shook his head and opened the bag. "Just cherry pie filling and pepperoni."

"Yum."

"We're going to make pie iron pizzas for everybody," Jana said.

"Sounds delish. But hold the cherries for mine." Tracy pointed to her car. "Anybody want to ride with me?"

"I do." Matt walked beside Tracy. "Hey, Lisa told Mom about a photo treasure hunt where you have to follow clues and take pictures. Isn't that cool? I think we should do that while we're camping. Somebody can write up clues and hide them and then…"

Amy watched and listened until he opened the back door of Tracy's car and his voice vanished. She looked down when a little hand tugged on hers. "Can I get a chocolate muffin?"

While so many parents dealt with children begging for things they didn't need, this little breakthrough thrilled Amy. "Absolutely." As soon as the answer passed her lips, she knew she had to amend it. "Absolutely you can split one with Matt." As Jana scrambled into her booster seat and fastened it herself, Amy tapped the adorable fake pout pooching out her bottom lip. "Do you know how much sugar you are going to consume in the next five days?"

The pout morphed into a grin. "Lots and lots and lots."

"Exactly." Amy got in the driver's seat and headed to Electric Fountain Brewing, a coffeeshop owned by the CSU band director. The café's jumbo muffins were delectable, but more than any six-year-old, or forty-eight-year-old for that matter, needed.

They parked next to Tracy. Jeff was just walking in and stopped to hold the door open for them. "Perfect timing," he said, stooping to kiss Tracy.

"Wait for me!" Robin ran toward them, sandals clacking on the sidewalk. "Talk fast. I have a chamber meeting in thirty minutes."

Jeff laughed as they headed to the counter. "I've only got twenty, but cramming too much information in too little time is part of my job description." He pointed at a table with enough chairs for all of them.

Amy took index cards and pens out of her purse, something she always carried with her now. Matt and Jana started drawing the moment they sat down, but she knew Matt's attention was as much on the adult conversation as on the comic he was creating.

"Everybody ready for camping?" Jeff asked, clearly trying to ramp up the suspense. Having grown up with three sisters, he had perfected the art of torture.

Tracy, who had perfected the art of not giving him the satisfaction of showing her frustration, said, "Since you're clearly not ready to dish, Amy has something to tell us."

Amy grinned at Jeff, who looked appropriately deflated. "I met Niesha's friend Lisa this morning." She explained the photo treasure hunt then showed them the picture she'd taken of the inscription on the drawing of the monument. "Lisa thinks Niesha wanted her to meet her there at four this afternoon, but Lisa saw Emmett watching her apartment last night, so she doesn't dare."

"But we dare!" This from the boy who appeared to be intent on his drawing.

Jeff jumped up to get their order when they called his name. "Hold that thought."

When he returned and passed out coffee, juice, and muffins, and they'd all thanked him for treating, Amy resumed. "Like Matt said, I think we have to dare, don't you guys?"

"Absolutely!" Tracy said, on top of Robin's "Definitely!"

"Wait a minute." Jeff held up the hand that wasn't cradling a latte. "I'm not crazy about the idea of you all putting yourselves in possible danger."

"I'll protect them, Uncle Jeff." Matt wielded an imaginary sword then chomped into his half of a jumbo chocolate muffin.

"I appreciate that, buddy. I know they're safer with you around, but... Seriously, you will be wise, right?" He addressed his question to his wife, then widened his gaze to include Amy and Robin.

"You know we're not going to do anything stupid with the kids along." Robin gave him a reproving look that didn't quite avoid being comical.

"I do know that," Jeff answered. "At least most of the time. Anyway, on to Fritz. I was asking Joanne, one of the librarians, about him when Maura Childs came into the library. Joanne motioned her over and asked if she had ever heard of Fritz Wolfram. Maura got this weird Cheshire-cat smile and asked who wanted to know. When I said I did, her mouth opened, and she looked stunned. She stared at me and just said, 'Ah,' like I'd just given her the answer to some big problem, then closed her eyes and clamped her lips shut exactly like Corbin does when he's trying to decide whether he should tell the truth. It was hard not to laugh. When she opened her eyes, she asked me how much time I had. We sat down, and she told me all about Professor Alexander Wolf."

"Who?" All three women spoke at once.

"Alexander Wolf. He was Maura's predecessor, the art history professor right before her." Once again, he paused for effect, in spite of Tracy telling him it was cruel and inhumane. "He and his son owned an art gallery in Stuttgart, Germany. When the Nazis started confiscating art, they fled the country, escaping through Switzerland. In 1936 they came here to St. Louis, where his brother owned an art gallery. The day he landed on US soil, Fritz changed his name from Fritz Alexander Wolfram to Alexander Wolf, and his son Johannes changed his name to John Wolf."

Now-familiar goose bumps danced on the backs of Amy's arms. Another puzzle piece. But why hadn't they learned any of this from Hyrum Fischer or Cameron James? "That's why we couldn't find his obituary."

Robin tilted her head. "But there was that picture of them with Otto in front of the gallery in the 1940s. It called them Fritz and Johannes."

"I think I have an answer for that too. Apparently, Fritz changing his name was a bone of contention with his brother, who thought he should be proud of the family legacy and refused to call him Alexander. Otto came to the States years before Fritz and, according to Maura, he either never believed the reports of Nazi atrocities, or he supported them."

"Wow." Amy had seen pictures at the Holocaust Memorial Museum in Washington, DC she could never erase from her memory.

"In fact, Maura thinks Otto was part of the *Amerikadeutscher Volksbund*. I'm sure I didn't say that right. It was also called the German American Bund, a group formed by expats in the thirties to extol German virtues and lobby for causes helpful to Nazi goals. They operated youth and training camps around the country and eventually had a membership in the tens of thousands. Maura said Otto knew Charles Lindbergh personally."

Amy remembered the sickening feeling she'd had in junior high upon learning St. Louis hero "Lucky Lindy," the obscure US Mail pilot who rocketed to instant fame when he made a nonstop flight from New York City to Paris, had advocated against going to war to save the Jews. Years after the war, Lindbergh was awarded a medal by Hermann Goering, head of the German Air Force.

"But Fritz—*Alexander*—Wolf didn't share his brother's sentiments?" Tracy asked.

"Not at all. He came here with plans of working with Otto and his partner at the gallery in St. Louis, but quickly changed his mind. That's how he ended up here in Canton."

"Did you learn anything about Johannes?"

Jeff grinned and glanced at his watch. "Perfect segue to the most important thing. Maura knows something about our Green Girl. But she has to check on a few things before she can tell us. She thinks by the time we get back from camping, she should be able to talk. And she wants all of 'the Allen girls' there." He wiggled his eyebrows. "Whatever it is, ladies, I'm guessing it's big."

Chapter Nineteen

On their way home, Amy took a detour in search of the house Hyrum had said belonged to the Wolframs…or Wolfs. Tracy had found it, but she wanted to see it for herself.

When the house on the corner lot came into view, she pointed it out to Matt.

"So that's where the guy who painted Green Girl lived? And somebody stole a statue out of his yard?"

"Yes." Now that she was here, she remembered walking past the house in high school, dreaming of the day she'd have her own old house with "character." Unlike the one with cantankerous character she now owned, the redbrick house had been beautifully maintained. Like Hyrum had described, the porch was adorned with intricately carved gingerbread woodwork. She could easily imagine an old black Chevy coupe parked in front.

As she turned the corner, she admired the trellises on the side of the house covered in purple clematis blooms.

"Stop!" Matt yelled. "Go back!"

Amy slowed the car and pulled to the curb. "What did you see?"

"There was a big board over a window."

Craning her neck to look over her left shoulder, she saw the board. "Maybe a window broke in the storm."

"Maybe," Matt said. "Or maybe somebody broke in."

Amy wasn't sure where Matt's own version of imagining was taking him, but there was no reason not to go along. She turned the car around. "Okay, supersleuth, let's get a better look." She slowed as they neared the backyard. Next to the window covered with plywood, what was likely an apple tree stood, partially charred. Anyone not looking closely would assume several branches had simply died. But one limb was blackened and pointing at the back of the house like a gnarled, ghostly arm. "Look at the tree," she said.

"Whoa." Matt's voice was hushed, as if someone might be listening in on their conversation...in a car with the windows up and air conditioner blasting. "You said Green Girl smelled like smoke, right? I got it! The painter guy stole it from Grandma Pearl and hid it in his house, but Niesha found out and she wanted it so she could get a bunch of money for it, so she used dynamite or C-4 or something to blast her way in to get it."

Amy grimaced. *Note to self: No more* MythBusters *reruns.* She took her foot off the brake, and the car crept forward. "Or, the tree got hit by lightning in the storm on Saturday."

Matt gave a guttural, villainous laugh. "Or maybe not."

Amy stepped on the accelerator and slowly rounded the corner. "If the fire department was called, we can find out."

"That's scary," Jana said, her voice almost a whisper. "Fires are scary."

"They can be. But they don't happen very often. And we have all sorts of precautions at our house, don't we?" As part of the requirements for fostering, she'd had to install smoke alarms in every room, carbon monoxide detectors on every floor, and attach a collapsible ladder on the window in Jana's room. She'd drawn a floor plan of the house, shown the kids the safest ways to get out, designated a safe meeting place in the yard, and had a home fire drill. She'd hated every minute of it, knowing the fear it would instill in Jana, yet understanding at the same time how necessary it was. "Let's not jump to conclusions. We have to be careful that we aren't seeing clues where none exist."

"That's not what real spies say, Mom." Matt spoke with absolute authority, being a "real spy" himself. "We need to suspect everyone and everything. I read that in a book about spying."

Amy smiled. She had no desire to burst his little sleuthing bubble. She parked in their driveway. "Let's get the van packed first, then we'll have lunch. Don't forget we have to make room for everybody else's stuff. It's only a half hour drive, so we won't need snacks and games in the car." She turned and looked at Matt. "One book should last you the whole week. And no electronics, right?"

"Moooom. Duh. Why would I want video games when we're going to be out exploring in nature and putting ourselves in extreme danger finding Niesha?"

Amy tugged the brim of his cap down over his eyes. "I think you're the reason Uncle Jeff is worried about us."

"Nah. I'm the protector, remember?"

Amy laughed. "Okay, ready, set, let the camping chaos begin!"

The doors flew open, and footsteps pounded on the porch. Amy sat in the car a moment longer, taking a final deep, calming breath and praying for direction and protection. For them—and for Niesha.

She stepped out of the van and was about to shut the door when a vehicle slowed in front of the house. A black SUV. Amy's hand flew to her throat.

This time, as it sped away, she focused on the details. Chevy Blazer. Tinted windows, front and back. The last three digits on the Missouri license plate with the wheelchair symbol was RW8.

This time, she was calling the police.

"This is *awe*some!" Matt crawled backward out of the tent. He had rolled out their three sleeping bags and hung a lantern from the center of the dome. Amy had to admit it did look cozy, if a bit crowded. She'd shared this two-person tent with her college roommate several times. But Keri was a petite, ninety-eight-pound woman who slept like a rock. Two wiggly children, both prone to nightmares and waking up crosswise in their beds, could be another experience altogether.

"It's three thirty," Amy announced. "Guess I'll be on my way." She didn't really want to meet Niesha alone, but she couldn't take the chance that Jeff's fears were founded. Did Emmett know about the mailbox? Could he have seen the sketch? Or followed her?

She'd taken a circuitous route out of Canton. With Tracy and Robin discreetly acting as lookouts, she was confident they weren't followed out of town. She had called the police and told them everything, starting with the first time she'd seen the SUV. She'd thought tinted windows in the front of a vehicle were illegal, but she'd learned from Sergeant Dale Leewright that all states but Vermont allowed medical exemptions. That information, along with the license plate, made her wonder if Emmett was driving someone else's vehicle or if he suffered from some kind of medical condition.

Enough. She'd done all she could, and now she had to let it go. At least for the next three days.

"I'll go with you," Tracy said, looking to Robin for confirmation.

Robin nodded. "The kids and I will set up cornhole."

"No!" Matt shouted. He looked crestfallen. "We have to come with you."

"Yeah," Kai said, stepping close to Matt in a show of solidarity. "You might need some muscle, you know?"

Amy couldn't help laughing, but she shook her head. "Sorry. Not this time, junior sleuths."

Matt groaned. "I just wanna see her."

A tiny voice came from the picnic table. "I wanna stay here," Jana said.

Robin stepped close and patted Jana's shoulder. "I'm with you, kiddo. It's you and me against the boys, okay?"

Jana grinned, and Amy sent Robin a nod of thanks. She hugged the kids, ignoring the looks from the boys, and ducked into the tent for her purse. By the time she and Tracy opened the car doors, Robin had all three kids engaged in unpacking the cornhole bean bag toss game. For the umpteenth time, Amy wondered how she thought, for even a minute, that she could do this parenting thing without her family swooping in to help.

Before she'd even backed out of their group site, Amy's hands were damp on the steering wheel. How was she going to convince Niesha that she could be trusted? As they drove out of the campground, Tracy asked if she wanted to chat, or needed the quiet.

"Quiet for now. I think. Maybe. I need to calm my nerves and figure out what to say."

"Okay. I'll be praying."

By the time they saw a sign for Keokuk National Cemetery, she'd had enough silence. "Okay, can't stand the quiet anymore. Say something."

"I bet I've been here on at least six cemetery tours with Jeff over the years. Think I've just about got his script memorized. Want to hear it?"

"Anything. Yes."

"Okay. Here goes. 'The Sauk and Fox tribes were the sole inhabitants of the area until settlers arrived in 1837. In 1842, a treaty was signed with the two tribes, forcing them to move farther west. The treaty would go into effect on May 1st of that year, so, at one minute after midnight on May 1st, a horde of settlers rushed in to stake their claims.' Blah-blah-blah…

"'Keokuk's position at the confluence of the Des Moines and Mississippi rivers made it an ideal location for transporting goods during the Civil War. During the war, four forts and five army hospitals were established in the area. The cemetery itself was originally part of Oakland Cemetery, until the city donated the land to the US government around the time of the Civil War. Six hundred named Union soldiers were buried here, along with twenty-seven unknown soldiers and eight Confederates who died in Keokuk as prisoners of war…'"

As they reached the black wrought iron fence with large concrete blocks securing each corner, Tracy's monologue slowed, then stopped. Row after row of white tombstones, stretching as far as they could see, inspired a sense of somber gratitude. Amy pulled the van into the older, western section dating back to the Civil War. The entrance was flanked by two block pillars, each bearing a black and bronze plaque with the name of the cemetery. The Unknown Soldiers monument was just ahead on the left. In a quieter, reverent tone, Tracy explained that in 1912 the Women's Corps of Keokuk had dedicated the granite pedestal topped with a soldier standing at parade rest.

Amy parked along the drive and looked around. Off in the distance she spotted a man on a lawnmower. Other than the low thrum of his engine and a cacophony of birds in the trees, the cemetery was quiet. No movement, no sign of another human being. Was Niesha hiding somewhere, watching? With a deep breath, she grabbed the small string purse that held her phone and slipped it over her shoulder as she got out.

"I'm keeping a close watch and the motor running," Tracy said.

Amy walked slowly, focusing on the monument. The only place a person could hide was in the wooded area to her left. She purposely didn't look that way. When she reached the monolith, she looked at her watch. 3:58. She stood, hands folded, trying to appear as unthreatening as possible. When the numbers on her watch changed to four o'clock, she turned toward the woods. "I'm Angel," she said, projecting her voice just short of shouting. She waited several more minutes.

A crack. Like a twig breaking. She zeroed in on the sound and thought she saw a shadow swaying slightly at the edge of the trees, but she couldn't be sure. She couldn't blame Niesha for being scared. "We just want to make sure you're okay," she called.

No more sound. She couldn't just leave with no contact at all. Then an idea hit. She pulled a small notebook and pen out of her purse. Her first thought was to leave her phone number, but what if it wasn't Niesha watching from the shadows? What if it was Emmett? Her next thought was to write down her site number at the campground. Still too risky. Finally, she simply wrote, *Same time tomorrow. Angel.* Maybe by tomorrow Niesha would have had time to make contact with Lisa, describing "Angel," and would feel safe talking to her.

As she looked for a place she could wedge the note, she spotted a rock at the base of the monument that appeared out of place. She picked it up and a folded piece of paper fluttered. On it was a drawing. An incomprehensible message, and a pencil sketch. Of a six-legged bug.

November 25, 1937

Happy Thanksgiving! We are hosting this year and it's going to be an exciting (or absolutely horrible) day! I told Mother I felt bad for Bess and her parents because they have no extended family living close, so she invited them to join us, and then she did the most amazing thing. She invited John and his father too! I don't know why they aren't having dinner with John's uncle. That's another thing John was mysterious about.

I do hope Bess will be on her best behavior. She has been in such a foul mood lately.

Well, I have to go make my pie filling. I am making John's favorite, of course, cream pie topped with blueberries. I'm also making blackberry dumplings. John says he has never had them, but I'm sure he will love them. I'll write again before bed, assuming the house doesn't blow up before that!

10:30 p.m. What a wondrous day! Bess was nice to everyone. Of course, I made sure she sat next to John so she would be happy. Maybe that wasn't the nicest thing to do to him, because she talked incessantly during dinner. Her mother wasn't feeling well so they left right after dessert, which was good because Bess was getting upset that John raved about my cream pie and blackberry dumplings. She would have blown her wig if she knew he ate another serving of each after they left!

While we did dishes, Mother said it is common for a woman to feel sick in the early months of being with child. I don't think I want to have a baby ever! Anyway, the most amazing thing was when Father and Mr. Wolf went and sat by the fire after dinner and talked for two hours. John and I listened in whenever we could. Father doesn't discuss the war with anyone, but there he was talking to a man who was once his enemy! They talked of friends they had lost and the importance of forgiveness. Mr. Wolf said it was so hard to leave his home, but he could not support a government that punishes people for believing in God. He and Father hugged when they said goodbye!

Oh! John has a fancy camera with something called a shutter tripper that lets him be in a photograph he is taking! He took a picture of our whole group. And he took one of me sitting by the fireplace...after Bess left. He is going to develop it and send it to Gänse.

Happy Thanksgiving and good night, dear diary!

Chapter Twenty

Stars spattered an inky sky. Sparks from their campfire drifted up, tiny orange embers that vanished as if they'd become stars themselves. It was almost ten. Robin nestled against Terry's chest, Tracy and Jeff held hands as they all gazed silently at the fire. Jana slept on Amy's lap while Kai and Matt roasted their third and final marshmallows. Amy hoped the sugar wouldn't keep Matt awake, but she didn't have the heart to end this memory-making night. The look of wonder on his face overshadowed all the questions and uncertainty of the past two weeks.

"Can we tell scary stories now that Jana's asleep?" Kai asked.

His father shot him a look of warning.

"What if it's not nightmare scary?" Kai pleaded, eyes on Amy now. "How about Cow's Head?"

"Your mother actually taught you that one?" Amy well remembered Grandpa telling that old Ukrainian folktale as they sat around a fire just like the one that warmed her toes now. She could almost replicate the tingle of fear that crept up her back, even after hearing it several times and knowing the outcome for Oksana, the Cinderella-clone heroine. She shook her head. "Go ahead."

"Knock, knock, knock." Kai's spooky voice had Matt hugging his chest with the first few words. "The sound echoed hollowly through the dark cottage. Oksana woke with a start, her heart pounding in fear. It came again. Knock, knock, knock..." When Kai got to the part about a bodyless cow head at the door saying, "I am cold and hungry. May I sleep by your fire?" Amy was afraid she was going to have to make room on her lap for Matt. And then, the story wrapped up with a happy ending and a moral of sorts. Compassion won over fear, and Oksana carried the cow head to the fire and fed it the last of their food. The next morning a trunk full of beautiful gowns sat where the cow head had been. When the wicked stepmother heard the story, she went out in search of the cow head, but when she found it, she was too lazy to serve it. By morning, all her gowns had turned to rags and her possessions to dust.

Matt collapsed against the back of his camp chair. "Duh."

"What's the moral of the story?" Jeff asked.

Matt stuck his tongue out at Kai. "That's easy. Don't let your cousin pick the scary story. I know a better one. Yellow Ribbon."

"No!" Amy, Tracy, and Robin yelled in unison. It had been a night much like this one when Grandpa told the story of the young bride who always wore a yellow ribbon around her neck...until she finally, tragically, gave in to her new husband's pleading to untie it. Amy could still remember the gasps as Grandpa held a flashlight under his chin and whispered, "And her head fell off!"

"Time for bed," Amy said. "Before you come up with any other brilliant ideas."

Matt grinned as they walked toward the tents. Amy settled Jana on her sleeping bag and laid a sheet over her. When she crawled over to Matt, he was still smiling. "Know what, Mom? Even with dumb cow head stories, this was the best day of my whole life."

It was Amy's turn to smile as she rejoined Tracy and Robin at the campfire. Kai had decided all on his own that it was time to turn in. Jeff spread the hot coals, and Terry gathered up marshmallow forks.

"We are blessed," Amy said as she watched the last of the flames die. The embers glowed red-hot, occasionally crackling or hissing in the otherwise silent night. If only she had the assurance these wondrous times would continue.

"Amen to that," Tracy said.

"Mm-hmm," Robin agreed.

Tracy patted Amy's arm, intuitive as usual. "You know, whatever happens, you are making a life-changing impact on those kids. They'll remember this trip forever. Think of the ripples this could have on their future. They know what family can be. They'll want that for their kids. Someday Matt will be sitting by a campfire with his kids, and he'll tell them the cow head story."

Amy smiled. As she wiped a tear, her phone buzzed. "Who's calling this late?" She pulled it out of her back pocket. "Lisa." Amy had left a voice mail for her after she and Tracy returned to camp. "Hi, Lisa."

"Hi. Sorry I couldn't get back to you sooner. Hope you were still awake." Her voice faded in and out with the poor signal, but Amy could still make out her words.

"Yep. Just sitting by the fire."

"So you didn't see Niesha?"

"No, but I think she was watching from the woods." She wouldn't share her fear that it might not have been her.

"What was on the note?" Lisa asked. Amy hadn't felt safe leaving details on her phone.

"It says, 'Talk to his' and then there's a picture of a bug. An ant."

Lisa was quiet for a moment. "His aunt! That has to be it. I met Emmett's aunt once. She gave Niesha and me a ride to work when Niesha's car broke down. She's really cool."

"What's her name?"

"Deb, I think. Yep, Niesha called her Aunt Deb. I don't know her last name. She lives in Canton. I'm guessing she's in her fifties, maybe sixties. She used to own the art gallery in town."

Debra Smith. Owner of Canton Art Gallery. The teen in Grandma Pearl's sixty-fifth birthday photo. Amy rubbed her arm. She needed a new name to call these goose bumps that were becoming a regular occurrence. "I know who she is. Are you okay with us talking to her? Anything you think I shouldn't say?"

"Just tell her I asked you to call."

"Are you okay?" Amy asked. "Do you feel safe?"

"Yeah. I'm staying with a friend, and nobody's seen Emmett on campus. God is in control, right? I'm trying to memorize some Bible verses to say when I get freaked out about things. The one I'm working on now is Isaiah 41:10. 'So do not fear, for I am with you; do not be dismayed, for I am your God. I will strengthen you and help you...' And... Um..."

Amy filled the silence. "'I will uphold you with my righteous right hand.'"

Amy smiled as her sisters kissed their men goodbye on Wednesday morning, then she continued setting plates on the checkered cloth covering the picnic table.

"Debra Smith is Emmett's aunt." Robin returned to the firepit and resumed her job of flipping pancakes. "I didn't dream that, right?"

Amy shook her head and pulled a bottle of orange juice out of a cooler. "You didn't dream it. Lisa said Debra used to own the gallery. Did she sell it?"

"The last I knew, she still owned it but someone else was managing it. Debra spends her winters in Arizona, I think. She hasn't been to any chamber meetings for quite a while."

"Think I should try to call her this morning?"

Tracy took a plate piled high with pancakes from Robin. "Maybe we should talk to the police first."

"Good idea." Robin stood and brushed off her knees. "Debra's an art dealer. She knew Grandma. Her nephew is looking for the painting stolen from Grandma." She seemed lost in thought as she walked to the table. "What if Debra is involved?"

Amy took the foil off a plate of bacon and called the kids to sit at the table. "Kai, your turn to pray."

Kai bowed his head and simply said, "Lord, thanks for good food. Amen."

"Well said." Amy speared a pancake and began cutting it in squares for Jana. "I've only had a couple of conversations with Debra, years ago, but I just can't picture her as an art thief. Get that...*picture* her?"

Tracy groaned, and Robin rolled her eyes. Matt covered his face with his hand. "You're hilarious, Mom."

"From all the CSI shows you watch, you know how often people say the bad guy is the last person they ever suspected would commit a crime." Tracy wrapped both hands around her coffee mug. "We can't discount her just because she's a nice person."

Amy swirled syrup over Jana's plate and slid it to her. "You probably know her best, Rob. Do you think she could be involved?"

"I don't, but Tracy's correct. The right reason—desperation, fear, protecting someone—could force anyone to break the law. Maybe her mother stole it in 1987, and Emmett stole it from Debra. What if you call her but don't mention Green Girl? What if you just tell her we're looking for Niesha and thought she might know where she is?"

"Good plan," Kai said.

"Yep," Matt said through a mouthful of pancake.

Amy met Robin's gaze, and they shared a proud mom look. "I'll call Sergeant Leewright right after breakfast."

As they ate, they planned their day. The original idea of hunting for Niesha was set aside, at least for now. Amy hoped she would show her face this afternoon. If not, perhaps she'd have some information to leave in a note.

When they finished, they cleared the table. Kai, who generally complained about household chores, jumped up and started washing plates in a dishpan filled with water warmed on the fire. When Matt picked up the dish towel and began drying, Amy and Robin both gaped. "Camping miracle," Amy whispered.

Amy checked her phone. She didn't have a strong signal. "Let's head to the pool. I'll try calling near the office."

As they walked, she scanned each campsite for a yellow tent or a red car with a smiley face bumper sticker. There were several campgrounds in the area, and Nauvoo State Park was less than half an hour away. They had no way of knowing where Niesha was camping, or if she was even still near Alexandria.

When they reached the camp office, Tracy took Jana's hand and they went to the pool, leaving Amy to sit in the shade in an Adirondack chair. She called the police station and was relieved to hear Sergeant Leewright was in. They'd known each other since high school, and she felt comfortable talking to Dale.

"Amy." Concern tightened his voice. "You okay? Did you find the girl?"

She updated him on everything up to last night's call from Lisa. "I'm thinking of calling Debra Smith, but I wanted to get your opinion first. Robin thinks we should just ask her if she knows where Niesha is and not mention the painting at first. I'm not sure I want to be the one to insinuate her nephew may be involved in something." She didn't mention the possibility of Deb being involved herself.

"Good point. Why don't you call and talk to her, but if you set up a meeting, let me know when and where."

"Will do. Oh, one more thing. There's a house on Clark Street a few houses south of St. Joseph's that has a boarded-up window in back. It looks like there was a fire there recently."

"Katie Mason's house. I never heard what caused it. What made you ask?"

Katie Mason. Why did the name sound so familiar? Like an echo from her past. Had they gone to school together? "How old is Katie?"

"Hmm. Midforties."

"Could she be a granddaughter of John Wolf, who lived there decades ago?"

"I'm pretty sure she is. I think she was a freshman when we were seniors. I know the whole family has been funding the arts for generations. She and Debra Smith are best friends."

Amy sank against the back of the Adirondack chair. She thanked Dale, then closed her eyes and rubbed her right temple where tension was starting to build. Were they just being led on some senseless goose chase? She knew better than that, knew God was in control, but the twists, turns, and upside-down loops of this ride made her feel off balance.

Emmett's aunt and John Wolf's granddaughter were good friends. Was that just a random fact, or did it all tie into the mystery of Green Girl? She tried to organize her scrambled thoughts before looking up the phone number for the art gallery. She had a tendency to talk too much when nervous, and that would not serve her well in this conversation. She took a deep breath, arranged her face in a pleasant smile, and tapped on the number.

"Canton Art Gallery. This is Katie. How may I help you?"

Katie. Katie Mason? Amy shook her head, trying to clear it. So many questions she'd like to ask this woman, but this was not the time. "Hi. This is Amy Allen. I'd like to speak to Debra Smith, please, if she's in."

"She's with a customer at the moment. I'll tell her you called."

"Thank you." Then, even though she knew she should just say goodbye, she didn't. "Is this Katie Mason?"

"Yes."

"I think your grandfather and my grandmother were good friends."

"Yes. They were. Maybe you don't remember, but I was the bratty little redhead your grandma forced you to play with at her house."

"Oh! Ghost in the graveyard!"

"Yes! I was so excited that I got to hide in the house I'd heard so much about from my father. He told me about the secret doors and the dark, scary staircase, and I was so disappointed when I couldn't find them. Oh, I'm sorry, I have to take a call. I'll tell Debra you called, and I'd love to chat more sometime. Bye."

Amy stared at the black screen. Secret doors? Scary Staircase? All part of a child's imagination…or something else?

Chapter Twenty-One

"Sounds like some big-time imagining, cousin." Robin sat between Amy and Tracy on the edge of the pool as they dangled their feet in the cool water while watching the kids.

"I don't think so." Tracy held her water bottle against her forehead. "Jeff's been champing at the bit to take a sledgehammer to the back of the closet in the room that used to be Aunt Ruth's. The closet is drywall covered with cedar planking while the rest of the room is still the old lath and plaster. He's sure there's a space between the outside wall and that closet, and he's pretty sure it extends up to the attic and down to the first floor behind the pantry and maybe even to the basement. I just couldn't justify demolishing something that was already finished when we have so much work to do."

Robin looked at Tracy with doubt in her eyes. "Did he ask Mom about it?"

"Yes. She encouraged him to knock out the wall. All she remembers is that there used to be a door at the back of her closet, but it was always locked." Tracy sighed. "Guess I need to quit standing in the way of historical discovery and let him have at it."

Amy squirted sunscreen into her hand and began slathering her arms and shoulders. "Most Victorian houses were built with servants' stairways. So here's a crazy thought. Katie's father told her about the staircase. So either he'd been in it or his father had told him about it. Remember sneaking in and out of the basement through the old bulkhead door? It was never locked. We don't know when the door in the closet got plastered over. What if, in 1987, there was still a way to sneak in and out of the house and someone in the Wolf family knew about it?"

Tracy looked at her with raised eyebrows. "Why would John Wolf steal a painting he painted?"

"Maybe it was his son, Katie's dad. He thought it should belong to his family, so he snuck in and took it." Amy put the cap back on the sunscreen tube and slid it into her beach bag.

"Imaginating," Robin whispered. "The newspaper article said there were signs of forced entry. If the thief knew how to sneak in, he wouldn't have to break in. And why wouldn't he or she do it when no one was home?"

Amy sighed. "Right. I did warn the kids not to start thinking everything is a clue. It just seems strange that I heard about a secret stairway from Johann—*John* Wolf's granddaughter right now." She bent her head, trying to stretch the tension out of her neck. "Anyway, help me sort this out. I feel like my brain is a tangled mess. John Wolf painted a picture in the 1930s. We don't know who the girl, *girls*, in the painting are. It hung in Grandma's house until it was stolen in 1987, when Elizabeth Blair was visiting Grandma. We have no clue where it was for the next thirty-five years. Debra Smith is in that picture we found with Elizabeth and Columbia in it, taken a few months before the theft. Then we find the painting at a flea market. We know Indiana Jones got it from Niesha. Niesha disappeared. Emmett was asking questions about the painting, and we know he's looking for Niesha. We don't know how Niesha got Green Girl. Maybe she inherited it or stole it from the original thief, and Emmett the security guard is a good guy trying to get it back to whoever he thinks is the rightful owner. The security company guy said Emmett got a job in Canton. Emmett is Debra Smith's nephew. Debra and Katie, John Wolf's granddaughter, are friends. What am I missing?"

"The fire!"

The voice came from below them. Amy hadn't even seen Matt, a foot away, hanging on to the side of the pool…and every word they were saying.

"He's right," Tracy said. "Green Girl smelled like smoke when we found it at the flea market, and there was a fire at Katie Mason's house right before that. Is that a coincidence?"

"Nope. It's arson."

Matt's serious, wet, sun-reddened face made Robin burst out laughing. Tracy joined her.

Amy simply stared, aghast. Was this boy really only ten? How did he know about arson? She lifted her foot and flicked water at him. "Go. Play. Be a kid. Enough sleuthing for today."

Matt gave his version of a spooky laugh. "Until we meet Niesha in the graveyard." He pushed off the side and swam a few yards then turned around, treading water. "You shoulda told her you'd be back at midnight. Graveyards are boring during the day."

Another splash of water from Amy's foot, and he was off to rejoin the game of Marco Polo with Kai and a bunch of kids they'd just met half an hour ago. More memories in the making.

If the day came that she had to say goodbye, she had to hang on to the belief that they would retain the memories of carefree times, of being surrounded by a loving family. In God's economy, none of this time, this love, was wasted.

Leaning back, she tried to focus on only the feeling of sun on her face and water tickling her ankles. For the next few hours, she would force herself into vacation mode for the sake of the kids. And her sanity. She would stop thinking about the one-eyed SUV, and Niesha hiding in the woods, and Dillon maybe wanting to be a father after all these years. She would stop the what-ifs from looping through her thoughts on constant replay. She would forget about Green Girl and Indiana Jones and Debra and Katie and John Wolf and fires and the feeling of being watched.

Sure she would.

"What's for supper?" she asked. Anything for a distraction. "We're in charge of the pudgy pies."

"Hobo meals," Robin answered. "We're each going to make our own."

"Yum. What's going in them?"

"Ground beef, potatoes, carrots, onions, and butter." Robin gave her a strange look. Because, of course, she already knew the answer. The foil-wrapped packets were a staple while camping when they were young.

"Can't wait." Amy sighed. She hadn't meant her exhale to be heard by all.

"Photo treasure hunt after lunch!" Tracy's cheeriness was clearly meant to change the mood. "I wrote out the clues on my walk this morning. I don't think it would be fair to make it a competition, so we'll try it as a group activity."

Jana dog-paddled over to them, floaties on her tan arms, water dripping from tendrils of wet hair. Amy bent and lifted her out to sit beside her. "Time for a snack? We're going back to camp for lunch in less than an hour, but this should keep you from starving until then." She reached for her beach bag, took out a package of strawberry fruit leather, and opened it for her.

Jana stared at the dark red strip of puréed then dried fruit that did, indeed, look a bit like leather. Was this another new experience? "Taste it. You love strawberries."

One bite and Jana was hooked. Her eyes held that look of wonder Amy would never tire of.

They sat in silence, listening to laughter, splashing, and "Marco! Polo!" The bathhouse door opened, and a pale-skinned elderly man walked out leaning on the arm of a young man with a lifeguard build.

"Probably what Hyrum looks like in a bathing suit," Robin said.

Tracy laughed then grew serious and sat up straight. "Why haven't we looked at Hyrum as a suspect? Emmett worked for the Wolfram gallery. Both Hyrum and Cameron James said they'd pay big bucks to get a hold of Green Girl. Why haven't we considered that Hyrum could have stolen it thirty-five years ago?"

Amy's feet stopped swinging. She was about to say Hyrum certainly hadn't appeared suspicious, when she thought of the black cane with the silver knob. Tracy's words replayed in her head. *"You know how often people say the bad guy is the last person they ever suspected would commit a crime."*

Hyrum Fischer very likely drove a vehicle with a handicap license plate.

"Treasure hunt!" Matt shouted as he chewed his last bite of hot dog.

"Nah," Tracy said, patting her belly. "I'm way too full to walk. I think we all need to nap for a least an hour and then—"

"Aunt Tracy!" Kai and Matt yelled together.

Amy winked at Tracy. "Guess we'd better get changed." She pointed to Matt. "Out of swim trunks and into treasure hunt clothes. You can have the tent first."

"Yes!" Brown legs swiveled off the picnic table bench, and he ran to the tent.

In ten minutes, they'd put food away and all were changed into shorts and T-shirts. Robin handed out water bottles, and Matt slipped his camera strap over his head. Tracy handed Kai the first clue.

Kai held it so Matt and Jana could see it then read, "When the north wind blows, the water flows."

All three kids looked at Tracy with confusion in their eyes. Tracy laughed and pointed to the sign for the Pioneer Trail. "Thataway."

The kids started walking and Tracy turned to Amy, a grin on her face. "Guess it yet?"

When the north wind blows, the water flows. She repeated it several times. Why would water flow when— "The windmill?" she whispered.

Tracy answered with a smug smile. "Better catch up with them."

They'd walked about a quarter of a mile when Matt yelled, "There!"

In a clearing several yards off the path stood an old wood tower topped with a wheel of rusted steel blades. In front of it was a redwood sign that read CARSON HOMESTEAD, EST. 1878.

Amy looked around. Niesha had photographed this. She'd been here.

Matt and Kai scrambled around the base of the tower, but it was Jana who triumphantly held up the index card she found taped to the back of the sign. She stepped out from the shadow and sounded out the words. "Stop and say hi to the guy at the Y."

They waited while Matt took pictures.

"Stay on the path," Tracy said, and they trooped on.

About a hundred yards down, they came to a Y. Two arrow-shaped wood signs pointed to SETTLER'S GULCH and MARINERS' COVE. Between the two paths stood a cluster of trees. Amy had to laugh as the kids searched the backs of the signs and ran a few feet down one path and then returned and tried the other. In their search for a small card, they were missing what she could see standing at a distance.

Finally, Matt looked up, and up, and gasped. "Whoa. Cool!" He pointed at the bear carved from a dead tree and nearly hidden by the undergrowth. They ran to it and found their next clue rolled up and wedged behind its fearsome teeth.

"Can 'ou canoe?" Matt read, adding an eye roll aimed at Tracy.

"Mariners' Cove!" Kai shouted. He started running, but Tracy reminded them of pictures. Matt took several, and then Amy asked them all to pose together.

Amy was walking slowly behind them, chatting with Robin, when a flash of yellow fluttering between the trees caught her eye. At first, she thought it was a bird, but it was too large. She stopped walking.

"What's wrong?" Robin asked.

"I think..." She took a few steps off the path, straining to see through the tangle of branches. And then she saw it. A tent flap, loose and blowing in the breeze. A yellow tent flap. How many people had bright yellow tents? "That might be Niesha's," she whispered. "You go on ahead. I'll catch up."

"No way. You go look for her. I'll tell Tracy to keep going with the kids, but I'm sticking close." Robin squeezed her arm, then sprinted up the trail.

Amy looked around for an easier way to get to the campsite than through the tangle of wild raspberry bushes. She didn't want to scare Niesha by approaching from the woods. After a few minutes she found a footpath that led from an outhouse to one of the campground roads. With a quick prayer for strength, she stepped quietly along the gravel. Tucked back under a pine tree, almost concealed from the road, was the red car with the smiley face sticker. Her breathing quickened as she approached.

There, sitting on one end of a picnic table bench, with her back turned, sat a young woman with a mane of dark curls. And a dragonfly tattoo on her shoulder.

Chapter Twenty-Two

Amy crept closer, then, keeping her voice low, she said, "Niesha? I'm Angel."

Niesha whipped around, her face a mask of fear.

"It's okay. Lisa sent me. And I'm a friend of Pastor Gary. I just want to talk to you." She took another step.

Eyes full of doubt, Niesha finally nodded. "Okay." She gestured to the opposite side of the table, and Amy sat across from her.

"First, are you okay? Lisa and all of your friends from school are worried about you. Do you feel safe here?"

Niesha shrugged. "So far. I think."

"Emmett doesn't know where you are?"

The mask of fear returned. "You know Emmett?"

"No. Lisa told me about him. Is he looking for you?"

She nodded again.

"Niesha, I'm going to tell you everything that led me to you, but before I do, I need to assure you that we're only looking for answers, and we want to help you in any way we can."

"We?"

"I'm here with my sister and my cousin. We all attend Pastor Gary's church."

"Okay." Niesha's fingers, nails chewed almost to the point of bleeding, gripped the edge of the table, as if ready to push off if she needed to run.

"A couple of weeks ago, the three of us went to a flea market in St. Louis…" As she told about finding Green Girl, perspiration shimmered on Niesha's top lip. Amy continued, telling her about the painting being stolen in 1987 and ending with seeing Emmett in Matt's video.

Confusion replaced fear. Niesha released her grip on the table and covered her face with both hands. "I don't know where he got it." She lowered her hands. Tears shimmered. "I d-didn't always bring my paintings to the market. Sometimes just pottery. But a couple of weeks ago I decided to grab a bin of my old, unframed work. Mine are all on watercolor paper. I didn't even notice the canvas one until I started unpacking at the market. When I saw it, I almost got sick. I'd heard Emmett talking to someone on the phone about the painting that's in the background. A painting of a girl holding daisies." Her shoulders shook. "I thought he'd changed. We were reading the Bible together, and he was going to go to church with me. I thought…but I was an idiot." She folded into herself and began to sob.

Amy stood and went around to Niesha's bench and wrapped her arms around her as the young woman cried. When her tears slowed, Amy gave her space and waited until she was able to talk.

"I called the police." She shivered and rubbed her arms. "I'm not running from them, just Emmett. If he stole it, I could be charged as an accessory for selling it. I was just so scared I didn't think about that. I just didn't want him getting caught with it. He has a key to my apartment, and he called when he couldn't find the painting. I told him I'd sold it, and he just…blew up. He kept saying I had no idea what I did. I've never seen him so angry."

"Did he threaten you?" Amy asked.

"No. But he kept calling and saying he just wanted to see me to explain. I was afraid if I saw him, I wouldn't be strong. I love him, but I can't help him get away with this." She dabbed her eyes. "I'm so sorry about everything. I'm glad you got your painting back. You have no idea where it's been all these years?"

"None." Amy pondered how best to pose the next question. "Do you think Debra Smith was involved in any way?"

"Deb? No! Not if you're thinking she stole it. She's just not… No. Never."

"Would she protect Emmett if she had information about him stealing it?"

Springy curls bounced as Niesha shook her head. "No. I mean, she'd want to help him, of course, but I'm pretty sure she'd turn him in. She's always quoting that reap what you sow verse."

"You're sure Emmett is still looking for you?"

Niesha sniffled. "Yes. I saw him. I was camped down by the river in Canton, and I saw his car."

"What does he drive?"

"A '68 Mustang. Silver. He's really into cars."

Not a banged-up black SUV. Amy felt her shoulders relax. Though that still left too many questions. "What do you think Emmett is after? He knows you don't have the painting anymore."

"I'm not sure, and I'm too scared to find out. I thought I knew him, but if he's the kind of person who could steal... I just...can't." Niesha rested her head in her hand. She looked drained and exhausted.

Amy patted her hand. "Do you have a phone?"

"No. I ditched mine. Ironically, Emmett wants to be a police detective. He watches police shows all the time. I was afraid he'd know how to trace my phone."

"Do you need anything? Money? Food?"

"No. I'm okay."

"We're in Group Site four. Three women, three kids. My brother-in-law and my cousin's husband are coming up tonight. We'll be here until Friday around one. If you need anything at all, please come over. Even if you just want to hang around the campfire with us."

For the first time, a tiny smile graced Niesha's face. "I guess I could use some company." She wiped her eyes with both hands and took a shuddering breath. "Your real name isn't Angel, is it?"

"No. It's Amy."

"Well, if it's okay with you, I think I'll just keep calling you Angel."

Amy stood, then bent and hugged Niesha. "There's no way I can live up to that name, but it's okay with me."

December 4, 1937

I baked snickerdoodles today and took some to Richard and some to John. I want to be a good friend and try to help John think of happy things. We sat outside even though it was chilly. He said I couldn't come in, because he is working on a Christmas present for me. I think that's not the real reason. I think he doesn't want me to see the secret door.

John showed me a letter from Gänse. It was kind of written in code. It sounds like a cheery letter talking about people they both knew, but John could read between the lines. In one sentence she said, "As you well know, there is nothing malicious about your favorite artist. Some people simply don't agree with some of his practices, and that makes life difficult for all of us." John explained that her father was his "favorite artist," and she was referring to the MPA, the Malicious Practices Act passed four years ago that gives the Nazis a reason to get rid of people they consider oppressors or enemies. That was when I found out what I had suspected. Gänse is Jewish. Under the Act, anyone who is not completely in favor of the Nazi ideology can fall into the "oppressors and enemies" categories, including poor people, those who are disabled, and Jews.

John assumes what Gänse means is that her father is being watched, making it harder for them to leave the country even though their papers are in order. At the end of her letter, she thanked him for what he had risked to preserve her family's legacy. John did not explain that, but he did tell me one of the reasons he and his father and the Sommer family decided to come to America was because it is now illegal in Germany for him to marry Gänse because she is Jewish.

I am afraid for my new pen pal and even more afraid for what it would do to John's heart if she can't come here. The later it gets in the year, the more dangerous an ocean voyage will be. What if they can't get out? I have been listening to the radio with Father every night now. He said Mr. Wolf told him that if they had stayed in Germany John would have been forced to serve in the Wehrmacht, fighting for a cause they do not believe in. He told Father he is sending money to friends and family, trying to help them escape. I think maybe Father will give him some money to send too. I remember when I was little and thought that because he was the bank manager, all the money was his. I wish now that was true. Dear God, please stop the evil.

Chapter Twenty-Three

On Thursday evening, Amy knelt on the ground next to the firepit, helping Jana hold their pie iron over the coals. Matt and Kai were making their own, and Terry and Jeff were each manning two. Tonight's menu called for Reuben pudgy pies. Amy and Jana were splitting one. Jana, not surprisingly, had opted for no sauerkraut on her half. Tracy and Robin were busy spreading butter and cinnamon on canned biscuit dough, then cutting it into strips to be wound around sticks, toasted over the fire, then drizzled with frosting. They'd gotten in a two-mile hike this afternoon, but Amy knew she wouldn't be stepping on the scale the day after they got home.

It had been a good day. Swimming, a trip to watch a barge go through Lock and Dam 19, and a hike along a bluff overlooking the Mississippi. Tomorrow they were heading to Nauvoo State Park. Amy had planned to use that part of their weekend to look for Niesha, but now she could focus on the kids and having fun. Niesha hadn't shown up at their campsite yet. Amy was disappointed, but understood. It must have been hard enough for her to open up and trust "Angel."

When the golden-brown Reuben pies were all on paper plates, Terry asked God to bless the food. Matt cut his sandwich in half, then picked it up, laughing when strings of Swiss cheese looped between the two halves.

They'd just started toasting their "cinnasticks" when a quiet voice behind Amy said, "Hi." She turned to see Niesha, holding a bouquet of purple coneflowers and bright yellow primrose.

The poor girl may have been overwhelmed by the welcome she received, but she didn't show it. After introductions were made, Amy put the flowers in a Mason jar and Tracy handed Niesha a dough-wrapped stick. "It looks like a caduceus," Niesha said. Looking at Kai and Matt, she told them about the medical symbol of two snakes wrapped around a winged stick. "It might have come from the book of Numbers in the Bible. When Moses asked God to protect the people from serpents, God told him to make a fiery serpent out of brass and put it on a pole. He said if anyone got bitten by a serpent, all they had to do was look at the pole and they would be healed."

"Wow." Kai looked at Niesha with admiration, and likely something more in his eyes.

"Awesome," Matt added. Firelight reflecting on his face as he gazed across the orange coals at Niesha revealed an expression that cloned Kai's. Amy repressed a smile. Was she witnessing a first crush?

They chatted about their hike and visit to the locks while savoring their gooey dessert. As she threw a paper plate into the fire and watched the flames curl and blacken the edges, Amy remembered something she should have asked Niesha. Edging close to Tracy, she whispered that maybe the men and kids could go for an evening swim to cool off before bed while the women cleaned up. She gave a slight nod toward Niesha as she said it. Thankfully, years of nonverbal communication meant Tracy understood.

After they left, towels draped over their necks and Jeff leading a round of "I Saw a Bear," the women finished cleanup and sat at the table. Amy looked at Niesha. "I thought of something I should have asked you yesterday." She kept her tone light. "When we found the painting at the flea market, it smelled like smoke. The man we bought it from wasn't trying very hard to protect his old maps and things, so I thought maybe he had smoked around the painting and it had absorbed—"

Niesha shook her head. "A couple of weeks ago Lisa said she smelled smoke in my apartment. We looked all over but couldn't find anything. But when I opened my bin of paintings at the flea market, everything in it smelled like smoke." She picked at a flake of loose paint on the table, then looked up. "Emmet was at my place right before Lisa came over that day. And she was there the day before and didn't smell anything." She chewed on a fingernail then seemed to realize what she was doing and dropped her hand. "The smell came from the painting. Does that tell you anything?"

Amy exchanged a look with Robin and Tracy. "It might. A few weeks ago, there was a fire at the house where the artist who painted it used to live."

The same look of fear Amy had seen the day before drained color from Niesha's face. "Do you think…Emmett started it?"

Robin placed her hand on Niesha's arm. "We don't know anything for sure. We're just trying to put all the pieces together."

Niesha nodded. Her eyes glistened with the tears she was trying to hold back. "I need to go." Within seconds, she sprinted away from their campsite.

Amy tiptoed downstairs in a quiet house on Saturday morning, passing her children's rooms en route to the kitchen. Matt lay sprawled across his bed with arms and legs splayed out like a flying squirrel. Jana snored softly, curled in a ball surrounded by her "lovies."

The living room was still littered with sleeping bags, duffels, and camping gear. She had mounds of laundry to do, but she would savor the quiet and her first cup of coffee on the swing as long as she could. It had started raining just as they finished packing up yesterday, another much-needed downpour that had thankfully held off until their tents were folded away. This morning, the grass looked green, and the air had a deliciously clean, rain-washed smell.

She opened her Bible and found the verse in Isaiah 41 she'd memorized. She'd gotten a text from Melanie on Friday saying Janelle and Dillon had promised to give her their final decision by the end of the month. Amy's gut had clenched when she read it, and she'd realized in that moment that she'd rather continue in the anxiety of not knowing than face hearing that Matt and Jana were going back to their mother.

In spite of her fear, she was determined to trust that God had a more perfect plan than she did for the children she now called hers. She closed her eyes and said the verse out loud. "'So do not fear, for I am with you; do not be dismayed, for I am your God. I will strengthen you and help you; I will uphold you with my righteous right hand.'" Then she went on to read the rest of the chapter, repeating verse seventeen and eighteen three times. "'The poor and needy search for water, but there is none; their tongues are parched with thirst. But I the Lord will answer them; I, the God of Israel, will not forsake them. I will make rivers flow on barren heights, and springs within the valleys. I will turn the desert into pools of water, and the parched ground into springs.'"

The ground in front of her house that had been parched was now turning green, a visual reminder that God would bring good things. It might not be what she longed for, but it would be for the best.

The screen door opened, and Jana came out, holding Piglet by one pink ear. She crawled onto Amy's lap and snuggled in. Amy held her, maybe a little closer than most days.

Jana yawned. "What are we doing today?"

"First, we're going to have french toast, then we're going to put all our camping things away and start washing clothes." Amy laughed at Jana's "yucky" remark. "Then, at noon, Olivia is coming over to have corn dogs and tater tots with you and Matt. Tracy and Robin and I have a meeting at the college and when we get home, we'll set up the water slide."

"Yay!"

Amy jumped when her phone, sitting on the arm of the swing, buzzed. Her pulse skipped a beat, only resuming normal rhythm when she realized it was too early for Melanie to call. Was this how she was going to react all week? The call was from Tracy. She picked it up and tapped the green button. "Hey, Sis."

"Hey." Tracy sounded like she hadn't been up long. "Hope I didn't wake you. Is your morning free?"

"If you have a better offer than laundry, it is."

"Well, it's work, but it's more interesting work. Jeff's been up since five trying to figure out if he should knock out the back of the closet or if there's a less destructive way to access the space at the rear of the house. Now he's thinking that huge armoire in the attic might be hiding a door. But there's so much stuff piled in front of it he can't get to it. Want to come help me?"

"Love to. That's way more interesting than dirty clothes."

In less than an hour, Matt and Jana were contentedly munching popcorn and watching *Homeward Bound* with Sadie in Tracy's family room. The nineties movie would likely result in a reprise of the "we want a puppy" refrain they'd started the morning after *The Stray*, but Amy had her defenses in place this time. Her goal was to convince them how much better it was to have dog cousins they could play with anytime but never had to clean up after. It was worth a try anyway.

Half an hour into their sweltering task in the attic, Amy shoved damp tendrils off her neck then pulled another cardboard file box off a pile of boxes hiding the old armoire. "If Grandma hadn't kept everything in the living area of the house so uncluttered, she and Grandpa might have been classified as hoarders."

Tracy laughed, then coughed as she hefted a box labeled *Bible Study Books* and a plume of dust floated up. "Dad said it was Depression and War-era frugality. That generation had it so ingrained in them to not waste anything. Were you around last year when Grandma caught me tossing out a few of those pink plastic basins from the hospital? She must have had fifteen of them."

"I was there. 'We might need those sometime.'" Amy used her best Grandma Pearl voice. Tracy joined her on the next line. "'Put 'em in the attic.'"

Amy stacked two boxes against the wall then went back to the barricade they were dismantling to open a path. Several framed pictures were sandwiched between the row of boxes she was moving and the row that pressed against the armoire. She lifted the first one. On the back were the handwritten words, *Pearl and Bess. JW 1938*.

Her breath caught. "Trace..." She turned it around and gasped.

It was a pencil sketch of two young women sitting on a bench, laughing. Just the top of one carved leg of the bench was visible.

"That's..."

"The same bench that's in Green Girl." Tracy finished her thought.

"Who's Bess?"

Tracy shook her head. "Why didn't we listen better when Grandma talked about her younger years?"

Amy stared at the painting, then at Tracy. "Bess is a nickname for Elizabeth! Good Queen Bess, Bess Truman..." She rubbed the small of her back. "So Elizabeth knew John Wolf too." Her gaze dropped to an empty frame that had been partially covered by the drawing of Bess and Grandma Pearl. The top edge of the carved wood frame was scarred by a crescent-shaped gouge. A bit of torn brown paper stuck out from the back. Part of a message was written on it. She knelt to get a better look. *Happy 16th B* and below it, *Pea*.

Tracy let out a long, loud breath. "Pull it out."

Together they lifted it and turned it around. The chills and bumps that raced up Amy's arms outdid any she'd felt before as she looked at the scrolled and gilded frame that had once held Green Girl above the fireplace downstairs.

They stood in silence for several minutes before Tracy found the breath to utter. "Why...?"

All Amy could do was nod mutely. Why was the frame for the painting stolen off the wall in 1987 here in Grandma's attic?

December 18, 1937

I'm sitting in my secret place. I don't want Mother walking in on me while I write this. The worst thing has happened. Bess and I went to John's house with Christmas cookies today and their housekeeper answered the door with a hanky in her hand. She could hardly speak because of her tears. Next, we saw Mr. Wolf. He was distraught and pacing the floor. All he told us was that there had been a family crisis. Bess tugged on my arm and said we should leave, but I could not. I asked Mr. Wolf if we could see John. He said no. Finally, Bess left alone. The moment the door closed behind her, Mr. Wolf said, "I am glad you are here, Pearl. My boy needs his good friend today. He told me that you know about

Gänse, and I am glad. We have just received a telegram informing us her father has been arrested." Then he dropped into a chair. Moments later, he clambered to his feet and led me down the hall. To the secret door.

I cannot write what I saw behind that door, but now I know what John did to protect the Sommer family's legacy. I have always thought John was an amazing man, but now I see him as a true hero. I will carry their secret to the grave.

John's hair was a mess, and his eyes looked frantic. He said Max Sommer is a wonderful person, but some of his paintings are controversial. He painted things depicting freedom, like children playing and dancing. The part that is controversial is that the children all have dark hair! That is so wrong! John said this means Gänse and her mother probably won't be coming, even though he knows Max would want them to come to America to be safe, even without him.

We talked for a long time. Mostly I just listened to him talk about how wonderful Gänse is. She was going to be a music teacher but now she can't because Jews are no longer allowed to teach in public schools. In some cities in Germany, Jewish children are not allowed to go to school. There must be something someone can do about this. Why doesn't FDR do something?

John is a very brave person, and I am honored that he trusts me with his secrets, but I feel so helpless. I don't know what to say to help him feel better. I read Psalm 91 to him. It talks about God being our refuge and fortress, that He will hide us under His wings like we are baby chicks, and we don't need to be afraid. I skipped over the part that talks about tens of thousands of people falling "at thy right hand," and went on to "There shall no evil befall thee, neither shall any plague come nigh thy dwelling. For he shall give his angels charge over thee, to keep thee in all thy ways."

I want to believe God will protect Gänse and her family, but it is hard to have that kind of faith, and harder still to believe that even when horrible things happen, God is still good.

Chapter Twenty-Four

Waiting for Professor Childs to come back to her office, Amy impatiently tapped her foot. Maura had walked in, set two books on her desk, and said, "I'll be right back."

"What's she up to?" Robin whispered.

"I don't know, but it has to be important for her to schedule a meeting with us on a Saturday. Maybe she—" Tracy never finished her thought because, at that moment, Maura returned, followed by Professor Douglas and a young man who appeared to be in his early twenties.

As they settled onto folding chairs, Maura introduced the young man. Zach Hartman was a student who was learning the skills needed for art restoration. "Professor Douglas and I have both spent a great deal of time with Zach," she said, "prepping him for spending his senior year in Europe, recovering and restoring works of art confiscated by the Nazis. When you showed me the picture of your grandmother's painting, it was all I could do to contain my excitement, but I could not share my thoughts until I had spoken to Zach."

"So you recognized it as a John Wolf painting?" Tracy asked.

"Well, yes, but..." Maura looked at Zach. "Tell them what you know."

"Not enough," he said with a rueful smile. "There was a house fire here in Canton recently—"

"At Katie Mason's home?" Amy interjected.

He nodded. "One of the pieces in her priceless collection, a painting of the Cologne Cathedral, was exposed to smoke in the fire. Katie hired me to work on restoring it in the studio at the Canton Gallery. When I removed the backing paper, I discovered what I immediately recognized as a crude pencil-drawn map of this town. But the biggest surprise came when I realized that there were *two* paintings in the same frame. A layer of acid-free paper separated them, protecting the one that I understand once belonged to your grandmother."

Robin and Tracy crossed their arms simultaneously, as if trying to hold in their excitement. Amy could feel the same sensation pulsing through her entire nervous system.

"When I removed the canvas from the frame and turned it over, I actually experienced a wave of shock. I recognized something in the painting of the woman in the green dress." He paused, making eye contact with each of the women in turn. "You see, last semester I wrote a paper about the lost art of Max Sommer, a Jewish artist who lived in Germany before World War II. He and his wife died in a concentration camp. They had one daughter. I wasn't able to find any record of what became of her."

A pang of sadness tightened Amy's chest as she remembered Hyrum's account of Fritz Wolfram's artist friend and his wife and daughter who died at Ravensbrück. Could it be the same family?

Zach opened a leather satchel and pulled out a sheet of paper but kept it facedown on his lap. "In 1936, a statue and twenty-nine Max Sommer paintings were taken from an art museum in Munich, Germany. In 1987, most of them were anonymously returned to the museum."

"Paintings that were stolen by the Nazis?" Robin asked.

"No. That's the interesting thing. From what I've uncovered, it seems someone broke into the museum and took only Sommer's work just days before the Nazis began confiscating and destroying art collections in that area."

Amy rubbed the bumps that popped up on the backs of her arms.

"Here is where your painting comes in. One of the seven that were not returned was one that Max painted of his daughter. *Gänseblümchen mit Gänseblümchen,* English translation, *Daisy with Daisies.*" He lifted the paper from his lap, showing them a black-and-white photograph of a very familiar scene—a little girl in a long white nightgown holding a bouquet of daisies.

Zach waited a moment, as if letting the significance sink in. Facts scattered in Amy's mind like a thousand-piece puzzle dumped onto a table. She struggled to sort them. Paintings were taken from a German art museum in 1936…a year before a transaction of some kind was made between then sixteen-year-old Grandma Pearl and a St. Louis art gallery for a painting that featured a piece of the stolen art. Then, in 1987, the year of the break-in and theft of Green Girl, many of the stolen art pieces were returned to the museum in Munich.

"So…" Tracy's brow creased, mirroring Amy's confusion. "John Wolf included a famous Max Sommer painting in the background of a portrait he painted of a young woman and that portrait hung in our grandmother's home until it was stolen in 1987. Now we know that, at some point, the stolen canvas was hidden behind another painting and has been hanging in John Wolf's home for…how long?"

"All we know for sure," Maura answered, "is that the Cologne Cathedral painting has hung in the dining room of the Wolf home since sometime after John's death."

Amy told them about finding the original frame in the attic. "It looks like the thief took the canvas but left the frame."

"Strange," Zach muttered.

"When you discovered it, and recognized the daisy painting," Robin said, "what did you do then?"

"I called Professor Douglas. It's a good thing the gallery was closed, because I think I was shouting. I mean, who finds a clue to a priceless, historic piece of art in Canton, Missouri?"

"You were definitely shouting."

All eyes turned on Arthur Douglas.

"I called Katie. She seemed simply intrigued until I told her about the Daisy painting. She said she had no idea there was a hidden painting. She gave me permission to talk to Debra Smith and Dr. Childs." Arthur's expression appeared guileless. In fact, his face shone with excitement.

"What did Debra say?" Amy asked.

"Not much, actually." Arthur seemed puzzled. "She was strangely silent when I told her, then she thanked me and asked me not to tell anyone about it."

"Debra came into the gallery a little while later," Zach said, "and just casually mentioned that she'd gotten a call from Professor Douglas. She looked at the painting, and I was sure it evoked some kind of emotion. Her voice got hoarse, you know? But she just thanked me for my work and handed me a check. I asked if she wanted me to come back to finish the cleaning process, and she said she would let me know."

What was that all about? Why wouldn't she have wanted him to finish the job for her friend? Was it because she knew the painting didn't rightfully belong to Katie Mason? "You were there alone while you were working?" Amy asked.

"I only do restoration work on Saturday afternoons after the gallery closes. A security guard lets me in…"

"Security guard?" Four voices echoed in the room. One of them Professor Douglas's.

Zach's head and shoulders jerked back. "Is that so weird?"

"Do you know his name?" Robin asked.

"Um… Yes. Emmett. Made me think of Emmett Brown from *Back to the Future*. Couldn't forget that."

Arthur ran a hand through his hair. "Was he there when you called me?"

Zach pressed his lips together. "I…don't know. He opened the back door with a key to let me in. I saw him leave. He couldn't have come in that door, because it opens right into the workroom. I guess he could have come in the front, and I wouldn't have heard him. But why would he? Wouldn't it have just been a coincidence if he came back when I made that call?"

After a few moments in which no one came up with a logical answer, Amy said, "You're pretty sure Debra recognized the painting? Or maybe the Daisy painting?"

"Yes. Very sure she knew something."

"Debra is a CSC alumna," Professor Douglas said. "She's quite an artist herself. She may have known John Wolf or known about

Max Sommer. I do wonder if she, or you, Zach, understand the historical significance of the portrait." He leaned forward. "Dr. Childs and I have been fascinated by the recovery of stolen Nazi art for years. After all these decades, there are still treasure troves being unearthed all around the globe. Your painting, right here in Canton, Missouri, may have just produced an extraordinary clue to the mystery of who returned the missing Sommer works in 1987, and quite possibly who took them in the first place. To think that collection could have been right here all those years…"

Amy sat back. "You're assuming John Wolf or his father stole the paintings."

"Not stole. Protected," Zach said. "Johannes Wolfram and his father came to the US in 1936. We believe they somehow pulled off a heist and retrieved priceless works created by a renowned Jewish artist and brought them here for safekeeping. In my book, those men were heroes."

Heroes. Amy thought of the man in the scarecrow costume. Had Grandma Pearl known all of this about her longtime friend?

Amy tapped her index finger against her chin. They'd held back details when they'd first talked to Maura about Green Girl. She couldn't think of a reason not to explain it all now. Like she had with Niesha, she started with finding it at the flea market and told them everything she knew. "We have reason to believe Emmett stashed the painting in Niesha's apartment."

Arthur ran a hand through his salt-and-pepper hair. "So we're right, and he must have overheard Zach on the phone." He looked at Zach. "We talked money, didn't we? I think you told me your guess of what *Daisy with Daisies* would be worth today. If Emmett overheard that and thought we were talking about the Emerald painting..."

"There's something else," Tracy said. She seemed unsure about continuing. Amy had a feeling she knew what she was going to say and encouraged her with a nod. Tracy pursed her lips, then said, "Emmett is Debra Smith's nephew."

Again, Amy studied faces, looking for the signs Matt had taught her. But there was no fidgeting or looking away. Zach and the two professors shared the same look of bewilderment.

"Oh." Maura shook her head. "That adds another layer of... confusion. If he took it, did she know about it?"

"That," Amy said, "is the next thing we—and by 'we' I mean the police—need to find out."

They shook hands and parted ways. As they walked out of the building into a blast of July heat, Amy held up her phone. "I'm going to call Dale and find out the exact day the painting went missing from the gallery."

The dispatcher connected her to Dale, and she waited while he accessed records from the laptop in his squad car. "Nothing reported," he said. "I checked from the date of the fire on. Sorry. I take it you haven't talked to Debra yet."

"Hoping to do that right now." She thanked him and said she'd keep him posted, then hung up. Turning to Tracy and Robin, she said, "Now I'm going to call the gallery and see if we can corner—I mean meet with—Debra right now. You both in?"

Two nods gave her the go-ahead. An employee named George answered, and she asked if Debra was in.

"I'm sorry, ma'am, she's out for lunch."

Amy considered asking where she'd gone, then decided that was a bit too prying. "Do you know what time she'll be back?"

"Well, ma'am, it's shrimp fajita day, so I'm guessing she'll be back a little later than usual. One-thirty maybe."

Amy thanked him and replayed the conversation as they walked to Robin's car. There were two Mexican restaurants in town. Which one would she choose? Likely the one closest to the gallery. "Los Nopales, driver."

Robin pulled out of the parking space. "Is this crazy?"

"Maybe a little," Tracy said, "but we won't interfere with her lunch for more than a minute. Or two. We only want to find out if she knows how Green Girl got from her gallery to Niesha's apartment."

"And where Emmett is," Amy added.

Tracy gave a short huff of a laugh. "And if she knows anything about Green Girl being stolen in 1987. Like I said, only a minute or two."

"But let's not tell her we found it," Robin said. "Let's let her squirm a bit."

Amy looked at her in surprise. "Says the girl who disdains CSI shows."

As they drove away from the college, Amy wrestled with doubt. "Let's decide when we get there. If she's alone, it's a go. If she's meeting with a bunch of people, or if it looks like an important business meeting, we can change our minds and just order tacos."

"Sounds like a win-win." Robin turned off Washington and onto Fourth Street, then found a parking space.

"Stay cool and calm," Tracy said, clearly teetering on the brink of nervous laughter. "Act like we're just here for the food."

Amy opened the front door and held it for Robin and Tracy. She may have looked chivalrous, but it was really just a way to stall the inevitable awkwardness.

It only took a moment to find Debra. She sat alone, facing the door. Amy assumed Debra would recognize one of them. Everyone knew Tracy the reporter and Robin, owner of Pearls of Wisdom. She should have gone in alone since she was the newbie in town. "Let's get a table," she whispered. "It'll look more natural."

Tracy knew the hostess, so she had no problem asking for the corner table…three feet from Debra's. Amy took the lead, right behind the hostess. When Debra looked up, it was instantly clear they'd been recognized. "Debra, right?" Amy said, holding out her hand. "Amy Allen. You're a busy woman. Can I steal just a moment of your time?"

Debra gave a strained smile. She looked toward the door with the expression of a cornered animal. "Actually, I'm waiting for someone. I only…"

Her voice trailed off as an auburn-haired, middle-aged woman Amy didn't recognize approached the table.

"Hey! You didn't tell me we were having a party, Deb! Introduce me!" The flamboyant woman pulled out a chair.

"Katie, this is Amy Allen. Amy, this is—"

"Katie Mason?" Amy stuck out her hand. "Glad to meet you… again."

To Amy's surprise, Katie reached out and gave her a hug. "I should have recognized you right away. You've hardly changed." She laughed. "I've been wanting to call you. Sorry our conversation got interrupted the other day." As she stepped back, she glanced over

Amy's shoulder and her mouth parted slightly. "Is that your sister and cousin?"

"Yes."

Amy stepped aside and was about to say something to get Tracy's and Robin's attention off the menus they convincingly appeared to be studying when Katie stepped past her and said, "Tracy? Robin? I don't know if you remember me, but..." When she finished explaining everything Tracy and Robin already knew, she arced her hand toward Debra. "Join us. We just ordered. Let's push our tables together."

Debra's expression wasn't necessarily unwelcoming, but she looked extremely self-conscious. Fearful, maybe. Because of what she knew they knew?

Their server took orders, and they spent several minutes chitchatting. Katie had lived in Texas for years and had only been back in Canton a few weeks. "The older I get, the less I can tolerate the San Antonio heat, so I gave my tenants notice and came back. Although this month has me thinking I jumped from the frying pan into the fire. Quite literally, since I did actually have a fire at the house."

"We heard about that." Amy leaned forward, showing concern by her body language, but also to avoid looking at Debra. She was sure her real intention would be obvious. "What caused it?"

"The fire chief was fairly certain it was electrical. It's an old house."

Fairly certain? Amy couldn't imagine feeling safe with such ambiguity.

"Did it cause much damage?" Robin asked.

"Fortunately, smoke alarms woke me up, and I'm only five blocks from the fire department. The curtains over my kitchen sink were burning when I got downstairs. The heat blew out the window and started a tree on fire. I got the inside flames out with my extinguisher and the firefighters tackled the outside. Thankfully, no water damage in the house. All they had to do was poke some holes to make sure it hadn't spread between the walls. The smoke was pretty much contained to the kitchen and dining room. That's an advantage to older homes with doors to every room rather than the open concept most people want these days. I had to get rid of all my plastic storage containers and pretty much anything that couldn't be thoroughly washed, because of the possibility of toxins. Deb, here, is supervising the cleaning of a painting that was hanging in the dining room. And that's an interest—"

"Katie." Deb's tight smile flattened. "I think that's what they want to talk about." She sighed and looked at Amy. "Is that why you called?"

"Yes."

Another loud exhale seeped from Debra as she glanced at Katie, then scanned the room. "Maybe we should continue this discussion somewhere else."

Chapter Twenty-Five

They sat at a large table in Katie Mason's newly painted dining room. They'd gotten their food to go, and Amy stood and cleared the table while Katie sat and stared at the photograph of Green Girl Robin had handed her. Her finger traced the square frame on the Daisy portrait. "A painting in a painting," she whispered. "So is the woman in the green dress also Daisy?"

"We don't know," Tracy answered.

"I don't either," Debra said.

"And it was stolen more than thirty years ago, and Zack found it hiding behind my painting, and then it disappeared again?" Katie rubbed her forehead where deep furrows had formed.

"Yes." Debra picked at a manicured nail and slowly nodded. "Let me fill in some blanks. I was a college student back in 1987 when Pearl showed up at our house in the middle of the night…" She smiled, knowing she had the rapt attention of her audience. "Let me back up. My mother and your grandmother were friends through church. When Pearl heard I was an aspiring artist, she introduced me to John Wolf. I was in my teens at the time. He became my mentor. Though he'd stopped painting professionally, he and his wife did enjoy working with young artists and encouraging their careers.

I often came here for our sessions. We would paint in the living room while Daisy played the piano."

"Daisy?" Amy gripped her chair seat. "From the painting?"

"Yes. John's wife was the little girl in the painting in Pearl's portrait."

"We thought...we thought she died at Ravensbrück."

"That's what the world was supposed to think," Katie said. "Her parents were killed, but she survived. A woman disguised as a nurse smuggled her and several other young women out of the camp in an ambulance. My grandfather was madly in love with her before he and my great-grandfather were forced to come here. Grandma and her family had planned to join them, but her father was arrested. Two years later they were all taken to Ravensbrück. After the war, my grandfather got word they had all perished. He was inconsolable until he returned to Germany in 1946. He had told Daisy that if they ever lost touch, he would go to a little footbridge near her home every year on her birthday at noon. He did, and she was there waiting for him."

A collective sigh filled the room.

"They married, and he brought her back here. She went by Daisy, rather than her German name, after she arrived here. I don't know the details, but I know they didn't want my great-uncle Otto to know who she was."

Debra nodded. "That all weaves into the end of the story I'm going to tell you. One day, I'd guess it was around 1985, my mother, Daisy and John, Katie's mother, Pearl, and Pearl's friend Elizabeth Blair were here after a fundraiser luncheon, all standing in the foyer getting ready to leave, when suddenly little Katie popped out of a door beneath the stairs, where I had never known a door existed."

Katie slid her chair back. "Follow me." She led them to the stairway they had passed when they entered the house. Katie pressed on a spot just below a black-and-white photograph of the Gateway Arch, and a camouflaged door sprang open. "Watch your head."

They stooped to get through the doorway then kept their heads down until they cleared the slanted ceiling created by the stairs. Amy gasped as she took in deep carpeting and uncountable tiny spotlights, some aimed at the few framed paintings that sparsely decorated the walls. The only furniture was a large padded round ottoman in the center. As her eyes adjusted to the dim light, she noticed almost imperceptible shapes, squares and rectangles lit by LED lights that were a fraction of a shade darker than the surrounding wall.

"When Katie came out of this room, we all saw inside, and John had no choice but to let us in on the secret he and Daisy and your grandmother had kept for decades. But he made each of us promise to never breathe a word of it to anyone."

Amy's hand slid over her mouth as she realized what she was looking at. Seven paintings hung in this cathedral-hushed room. When she saw Robin's mouth open, she turned. And came face-to-face with *Daisy with Daisies,* a picture she'd only seen in miniature until now.

Debra gestured at the ghostlike images where frames had once been. "The walls were covered back then. Filled with the Max Sommer paintings John and his father risked their lives to protect."

Katie motioned them to sit on the ottoman. "Grandpa John and my great-grandpa Alex broke into a museum in Munich at the request of my other great-grandpa, Max Sommer. They'd gotten word through the resistance that the Nazis were going to start confiscating art in Munich. As you probably already know, Hitler began systematically acquiring the most desirable art pieces in Europe in the 1930s in order to establish a great museum in his hometown of Linz, Austria. He sought to fill it with the most 'culturally valuable' pure Northern European art. He and his officials also targeted modern degenerate art, meaning anything that either depicted Jewish subjects, was critical of Germany, or contradicted the Nazi ideology.

"With the help of a resistance fighter who worked at the museum and was able to shut off the power in the middle of the night, Grandpa John and his father broke into the Munich Museum and took every piece of Max Sommer art. They were both shot at and almost killed as they crossed the border into Switzerland in a bakery truck, but they survived and finally made it to St. Louis."

"Only to find out that Alexander's brother, Otto, was a Nazi sympathizer who was hiding stolen art *for* the Nazis," Debra said. "They had hoped to work, and hide the paintings, at his gallery there in St. Louis, but had to make other plans. Alexander secured a position as art history professor at CSC and they moved here. The paintings were safe…until Elizabeth Blair found out about them."

Katie gave a small gasp. "I… I didn't know there were any repercussions. What did she do?"

"Nothing…until two years later. Daisy passed away shortly after the day we found out about this room. And Elizabeth began visiting Pearl more frequently. Much more frequently." Debra's gaze took in Amy, Tracy, and Robin. "And then, your grandfather died. That's when the real trouble started."

Amy tried to guess where the story was leading, but nothing was making sense.

"Some of this I only pieced together in the past few days. My mother is eighty-six. She's in a memory care facility. One of the things that is fading along with her memories is her verbal self-restraint. After Zack discovered the hidden painting, I asked Mother for details surrounding the night Pearl showed up at our house. She had some long lucid stretches this week and had nothing kind to say about Elizabeth. Anyway, the story I heard was that Elizabeth, who'd been infatuated with John since high school, made an advance of some sort toward him and was 'summarily rebuffed.' Assuming the newly widowed Pearl was the reason he rejected her, she decided to get even. With both of them."

Debra closed her eyes as if giving herself a moment to get all of the facts in order. "In 1985, several European countries began publishing inventory lists of works of art that were confiscated by the Nazis in World War II. As a result, the Munich Art Museum joined many others in offering rewards for returned art. Elizabeth evidently saw this as her opportunity, but she needed an ally. Otto Wolfram's second wife, Ursula, was known as a ruthless gold digger. Otto was her third husband. After he died, she was devastated to find out the only thing he had left to her was a struggling art gallery and a ton of debt. Elizabeth couldn't have found a more perfect person to use in her scheme."

"Elizabeth told Ursula about the paintings?" Katie looked devastated. "I didn't know any of this. I feel terrible."

"You were a little girl. You weren't responsible for any of what happened." Debra patted Katie's hand. "Actually, I should say you weren't responsible for what *almost* happened. In fact, because of you, all turned out just fine. You see, these bitter, diabolical women had a twofold plan. Ursula wanted the reward money. Elizabeth wanted to get back at John. So Ursula paid a weekend visit to John, under the pretense of making amends. While she was visiting, she got into this room and took photographs which she and Elizabeth then sent to the Munich Art Museum and Elizabeth's contacts in the CIA, expecting John would be charged with theft and they would get the reward. That's where you come in." Debra nodded at Katie and grinned.

"The one thing those two schemers did not know was the secret of your bloodline. All John had to do was show the authorities the letter from Max asking Fritz and Johannes Wolfram to retrieve his work from the museum, and offer them proof that you were Max's only living heir and therefore owner of his collection, and that was the end of that."

Katie sat back with a sigh. Amy leaned forward at the same time. "But how does our painting fit into the story?"

"That," Debra said, "was a direct result of nothing going the way Elizabeth had planned. Every year, she came to help Pearl get the house ready for the tour of homes. Without telling Pearl, Elizabeth invited a reporter from a St. Louis newspaper to write a story exposing what John and his father had done. Meaning, exposing them as Nazi criminals, not the heroes that they truly were. The reporter was there, taking pictures of the Emerald painting when Pearl came home from a meeting. Elizabeth had timed it all so that her contact at the CIA would call right then and she would be the one to break the news of the legal action that would be taken against John.

"The call came, and it was not the news she'd hoped for. When she heard that nothing was going to be done to hold John accountable for taking Max's paintings and there would be no reward, that was the last straw. In Elizabeth's mind, Pearl always got everything she wanted, and she was always left with nothing. The way Pearl described it to my mother, Elizabeth 'went berserk,' and told Pearl everything she and Ursula had plotted, and then the focus of her ire turned to the painting. She screamed at Pearl, saying nothing had changed since they were girls. Then she picked up a leaded glass vase and hurled it at the painting. The reporter intervened, literally restraining her, and Pearl told her to go upstairs and pack her bags because she was leaving first thing in the morning.

"And that brings me to where I started. Mother and I woke to pounding on our door in the middle of the night. I had never seen Pearl angry, but she sure was that night. She held out the canvas and said, 'Hide this so it doesn't get destroyed.' She said she couldn't trust Elizabeth not to find it if she hid it at her house. We had just opened the gallery, and Pearl knew Mother would protect it. Then she went home and put scratches on her front door handle to make it look like someone broke in and told Elizabeth it was stolen because of her betrayal."

"That's why Elizabeth believed the reporter had taken it," Amy said.

Robin held up one finger. "The newspaper article said that Elizabeth was the one to report the painting missing. Now it makes sense why Grandma wouldn't have called the police. She wouldn't want anyone investigating."

"And we know now why she asked Pastor Gary about Corrie ten Boom," Tracy added. "She had to lie to the police about the forced entry to protect John."

"But Elizabeth being Elizabeth had to push it. She likely saw it as another way to get back at Pearl, drawing attention to something that, for once, hadn't gone her way." Debra paused a minute, staring at the Daisy painting. "Until this week, I hadn't thought of that night in several years. I had no idea where Mother had hidden the Emerald painting. The Cologne Cathedral picture it was hiding behind was another one of John's that had hung in our gallery before that night and for decades after. I gave it back to the family after John died, and they displayed it at his funeral."

"And then hung it in the dining room," Katie said, looking bewildered.

Deb nodded. "Your *Study in Emerald Velvet* was right here all that time." She looked down at her fingernails.

"But now it's gone," Katie whispered.

They went back to the dining room table and Katie served lemonade. Though she and Debra seemed unaware of it, the tension in the room was building. Amy, Robin, and Tracy exchanged looks. Who would be the first to address the elephant in the dining room?

"Who returned the paintings to Germany?" Tracy asked. A safe place to start.

"Grandpa John," Katie said. "After my grandmother died, he kept the ones he couldn't bear to part with and returned the rest to the place they belonged, in honor of his father-in-law. Now I wonder if it wasn't that he feared Great-Aunt Ursula or Elizabeth Blair might harm them."

They sat in silence for several minutes. When Amy felt she might snap like a rubber band, she said, "Debra, we have the Emerald painting."

She'd expected shock. Instead, Debra held her gaze. "I know." After a moment, she looked down. "Thank God."

What? As the word formed in Amy's mind, Katie said it out loud. "What do you mean? How did you get it?" She turned from Amy to Debra. "What's going on?"

"Did Emmett take it?" Robin's question was posed gently.

"Yes." Debra seemed suddenly infused with strength. Her shoulders straightened. "But not for the reason you're probably thinking." She wrapped both hands around her glass and took a deep breath. "I made a huge mistake. When I found out Zack had found another painting behind the cathedral, and he recognized *Daisy with Daisies* in the background, I immediately called my mother. She confirmed that she had hidden it and then said that Cameron would be delighted to hear we'd found it."

"Cameron James? Manager of the Wolfram and Randulph Gallery?" Tracy's surprise matched Amy's.

"Yes. Several years ago, as Mother was just beginning to lose some of her faculties, she and I visited his gallery. I left her alone for several minutes while I took a call. She'd been studying one of John's paintings. When I returned, she was deep in a conversation with Cameron." Debra closed her eyes. "I interrupted them and steered her away, but by then she had already told him about your grandmother bringing her painting to us in the middle of the night. Thankfully, she couldn't remember where she'd hidden it."

Debra took a sip of lemonade. Her previous stamina seemed to be draining away. "When she told me Cameron would be thrilled to hear we'd found it, I gave her strict orders not to call him. That man cannot be trusted. But within ten minutes he called, offering an exorbitant figure for Pearl's painting. When I said it wasn't ours to sell, he hung up. I wouldn't put anything past him. We have state-of-the-art security systems, but I was afraid if it was anywhere in the building, he might use threats or…" She rubbed her hand over her eyes. "I didn't have time to think. I panicked and called Emmett and told him to hide it while I figured out what to do next."

Tracy put a hand on Debra's arm. "And he hid it in Niesha's apartment."

Debra nodded. "When she told him she'd sold it, we both got scared. I know I should have called one of you." She raised her head to look from Tracy to Robin and then Amy. "When Emmett told me what he'd learned from the man Niesha sold it to, I knew it was the Allen girls. I'd been praying and praying for a way out, a way to protect Emmett. Who but God could orchestrate such unbelievable timing?" She looked away. "I'd hoped nothing more would come of it, but then Niesha disappeared, and we heard you were looking for her and…" Her eyes reddened. "It looked so bad for Emmett. I didn't think anyone would believe our story. He's made some big mistakes, but God's got a hold of his heart now, and he truly loves Niesha. We just need to find her and tell her the truth and—"

Amy reached across the table and touched Debra's hand. "We found her."

Chapter Twenty-Six

Amy paid Olivia for babysitting and walked her to her car. As she pulled out of the driveway, an all-too-familiar vehicle stopped on the street in front of the house. Amy's blood ran cold, and she reached for her phone. The SUV's door opened. For the first time, she got a look at the person in the passenger seat.

A woman, probably in her sixties, with bedraggled shoulder-length hair. She swiveled, lifting one leg, then the other, with her hands, then picked up a cane and slowly exited. A man, heavyset and wearing almost black-lensed sunglasses, came around from the driver's side and helped her.

Amy's pulse sped up. Who were these people? They couldn't possibly present a threat, could they? Why had they been stalking her? Slowly, she walked toward them.

"Are you Amy?" the woman asked.

"Yes." She barely heard her own voice. After clearing her throat, she answered again. "I'm Amy."

"I'm Martina Rundel. This is my husband, Frank."

Rundel. Amy's eyes widened as she remembered Melanie's account of the accident that had injured Dillon Rundel's parents. "You're Jana's grandparents?"

"Yes." Frank held up a hand. "I'm sorry if we've scared you. The police contacted us. We never had any intention of frightening you. We just…" His voice grew hoarse.

"We just wanted a glimpse of her. Dillon is facing the biggest decision of his life. We know we can't interfere, but she is our granddaughter." A tear slid down Martina's face.

Amy's taut muscles gave way as her fear morphed into compassion. Should she call Melanie? What would she advise? Before she had a chance to decide, the screen door slammed behind her.

"Oma! Opa!" Matt cried. "Jana, it's your grandma and grandpa!" He ran toward them, then slowed and gave each a gentle hug.

Amy turned. Jana stood on the porch, hugging Piglet. Amy held out a hand to her. "It's okay, Sweetie."

As Jana slowly stepped nearer to her, it was as if a dim memory gradually came into focus, and she smiled shyly.

Amy watched with pride—and a fear she dared not voice—as Jana walked into the embrace of people who were her blood relatives.

No matter how things turned out, Amy would make sure these people stayed in Jana's life.

"Many hands make light work," Robin said, quoting one of Grandma Pearl's favorites as she closed the door on the now empty armoire on Saturday evening. With Jeff and Terry's help, they'd finally cleared the path and found room for the fourteen boxes of record albums that had filled the antique cabinet.

"Time for the muscle," Amy said, stepping aside and motioning for Matt and Jana to take a safe perch atop a wooden trunk. Her gaze lingered on them for a moment, and then she repeated the words that had run through her brain on a continual loop since the Rundels left her house without giving any hint at what their son might decide. *God is in control. His plan is perfect. God is in control....*

Jeff struck a weightlifter pose then grasped one side of the armoire while Terry and Kai took the other. After a few grunts and groans, Jeff yelled, "Stop! We need reinforcements."

"This is deflating," Terry said. "How in the world did they get this thing up here?"

Tracy copied Jeff's macho pose. "Let's show 'em how it's done, ladies."

The women moved in to help. With all six of them pulling and shoving the massive piece, they inched it away from the wall.

"A door!" Matt yelled. "Uncle Jeff was right!"

"Was there ever any doubt?" Jeff jiggled the white glass knob of a rustic plank door with black iron hinges as the rest of them stood around, holding a collective breath.

A click reverberated through the attic, and Jeff pulled, almost landing on Tracy as the door opened and he stumbled back.

Cavernous darkness and the smell of must and stale air greeted them. Terry aimed a giant flashlight at the opening, and Jeff picked up a trouble light he'd plugged in across the room. The orange extension cord snaked behind him. "I know I should say ladies first, but I'm an old-fashioned guy. Just let us make sure it's safe." He found a nail and hung the light, then switched on his own flashlight.

As the men disappeared into the shadows, Amy held her hand out to keep Matt and Jana from jumping off the trunk, then moved closer with Tracy on one side and Robin on the other. They listened to the creaking of old wood and an occasional "Wow!" and "This is so cool!" Finally, Terry emerged with Jeff just moments behind him.

"It's steep, but there's a railing," Jeff said. "We need to hang more lights before the kids explore." He laughed when Matt and Kai gave simultaneous disappointed huffs. Sweeping his hand out, he ushered the women toward the abyss. "Go down to the next landing. It's at the door to the closet I wanted to open." His lips puckered and he stuck his chin out at Tracy in an "I told you so" gesture. "There's something on the back wall you need to see."

Flashlight in hand, Amy grasped the handrail and slowly descended. Grooves in the worn treads beneath her feet whispered of years gone by. As she, Tracy, and Robin stepped onto a small landing, she aimed the light at the back wall.

About two feet above the floor, she could just make out words written in pencil on an unpainted board.

PEARL'S PLACE
DECEMBER 25, 1934
MATTHEW 6:6

Tracy ran her fingertips across the words. "It's the verse about going into your closet to pray in secret."

Amy knelt by the wall. "She would have turned thirteen the day she wrote this." She scanned the small landing, imagining a young Grandma Pearl sitting in here and praying. There might have been a little bit of light from the closet, but there were no windows. "Brave girl."

Grandma had told all of her granddaughters that she started praying for them when she was young because a Sunday school teacher told her students to start praying for their future spouses, children, and grandchildren. Amy pressed her hand flat against a board to support herself as she tried to stand in the cramped space. The board moved.

Dropping back to her knees, Amy handed the light to Tracy and continued to put pressure on the board, sliding it to the right.

The flashlight beam illuminated a wooden box, about a foot wide and six inches deep. "Looks like a jewelry box," she whispered. Maneuvering so she could lift it with both hands, Amy grasped the sides and carefully extricated it, then she set it on the floor. Tracy knelt beside her. Holding her breath, Amy tried the small silver button. It slid and the latch popped open. Amy slowly lifted the cover, revealing a leather-bound red book with gold letters spelling out *My Diary*.

"Take it up, so we can see it in the light," Robin said, her voice hushed with awe.

When they stood under the bare bulb hanging overhead, with the last of the day's sunlight struggling through dusty, stained-glass windowpanes, Tracy held the box and Amy lifted the book and handed it to Robin. Beneath it were two more.

"This one is from 1938. No." Amy carefully turned a page. "It starts on Christmas Day in '38, so it's really '39."

Jeff found a piece of plywood and set it on boxes for a makeshift table. They lined up the books on it.

Amy picked up the next journal, this one covered in light teal blue with the same gold lettering on the front. She opened to the inside cover. *To our birthday girl. Love, Mother and Father. December 25, 1937.*

With shaky breath she read the first entry.

December 25, 1937

I am sixteen! I will tell you about our day but will save the very best for last. I woke this morning with a sense of disbelief. I feel exactly the same, and yet I don't. Maybe it's not the days I have lived this year, but the secrets I have been entrusted with that make me feel older. Maybe it is the knowing that my experience of living in a safe little world surrounded by friends and family is not the reality of so many girls my age.

Mother and Father served me breakfast in bed this morning. Pancakes with sweetened whipped cream and maple syrup. We talked about my tenth birthday and how Mother cried because there was no syrup or sugar in the house, and how she gave me her pearl ring because they couldn't afford anything new. When Father prayed over me this morning, I could hear the fear in his voice. I know he was thinking we could be facing much worse than we did in 1931 if Hitler has his way. Mr. Wolf has been telling Father things he learns in correspondence with friends in Austria, things Father says he does not hear on the radio. Mr. Wolf thinks Hitler is going to take over Austria.

On to happy things! I received this, the most beautiful diary I have ever seen! I love the ocean blue and the gold letters, and there are no dates or tiny squares for each day, so I can write to my heart's content on these smooth white pages!

We celebrated Christmas at Grandma and Grandpa Wallace's. So much good food, and my stocking was bulging with candy and nuts and two oranges! Where do oranges come from at Christmas?

On to the best news! John and Mr. Wolf invited us to their house for lebkuchen, the most delicious ginger cookies I have ever tasted. Then he showed Father the things I already knew about. Mr. Wolf asked us to please not tell anyone. He said he trusted us and wanted to be sure that if something happened to him, someone would help John protect their secret. It sounded like words from a spy novel, and it scared me. He explained that after he and John moved to St. Louis, he discovered that his brother, Otto, had joined a group of Nazis there. I could not believe my ears when he said this. How is this possible? Why would someone living in America want to follow that evil man? Anyway, he is afraid of what those people might do to him if they were to find out he has artworks that should be destroyed because they were painted by a Jew.

Thankfully, the night ended on a happy note. John and Mr. Wolf brought out a giant package wrapped in brown paper. I was so excited. I knew it was one of John's paintings, but I was not prepared for what I saw when I unwrapped it. There before me was a portrait of me! John painted me sitting in my green velvet birthday dress, the one I wore today. I am sitting on a bench looking at the picture of Gänse holding a bouquet of daisies. Later, John said he painted what he treasured most. I started crying. Then John handed me a check! He said the portrait was for my parents, but a model must be paid a sitting fee, even if she did not know she was a model. Though the paper clipped to the check said it was from Wolfram & Randulph Fine Arts and looked all official, the check was from John's account. This was his plan all along to help me buy my RCA Victor!

I'm trying not to think about what Bess will say when she sees the painting of me in the dress that matches hers. I'm afraid there will be an awful scene. I wish Gänse would come so Bess can finally leave her designs on John behind. But I will not think any more of this tonight!

Mr. Wolf told Father he would understand if he was afraid to hang the painting, considering Otto might find out, but Father said, "You, Alex, have shown me what freedom is *truly worth. We will not live in fear." When we got home, he hung my picture above our mantel. So now, as I sit here, my prayer is the same. Almighty God, may we, and my future children and their children for generations to come, never have to live in fear.*

Chapter Twenty-Seven

Dish towel slung over her shoulder, Amy walked back into the kitchen that smelled like it had on so many Sundays when Grandma Pearl reigned over their family dinners. Tracy had asked her to pick the menu for her birthday dinner and she'd requested blackberry dumplings instead of cake. When her sister had insisted Amy was the only one who could make them as good as Grandma Pearl, she'd found herself cooking part of her own birthday meal. She checked the dumplings, slowly simmering on the stove. "I'm calling it," she told Tracy and Robin.

"I'll get the ice cream," Tracy said.

"And I'll grab the bowls and a ton of birthday candles," Robin added.

"I'll summon the troops." Amy walked into the living room, thinking how wonderful it was that walls that had once absorbed the laughter and chatter of three little girls now resounded with the giggles of another generation. She smiled at Anna and Sara, who'd been ordered to put their feet up after dinner and watch the kids. Their new Sunday dinner guest sat on the oval braided rug in front of the fireplace. Corbin and Emerson gave Niesha their undivided attention as she read to them. Next to her, in a completely uncharacteristic move, Kai built a tower of blocks for Aiden. Matt looked proud holding a sleeping Zoe. An hour earlier, she had toddled up to him, handed him her fuzzy pink blanket, and nestled on his lap. Another first, Amy was sure. And again, she fought the wave of what-ifs.

In one corner, Emmett laughed with the men, entertaining them with a tale from one of his security jobs. Amy smiled at the sight then turned to head back to the kitchen when her phone buzzed in her apron pocket.

She stared at the screen, forgetting for a moment what to do next.

Melanie would never call on a Sunday unless it was something serious.

Please, God, no. Not today. No bad news on my birthday. But would there ever be a good day to hear the news that would carve out a chunk of her heart? Shaking, she tapped the screen and answered.

"Amy! Amy! Amy! I couldn't wait until tomorrow to call you. Janelle just called. She is relinquishing all parental rights to Matt and Jana. She and Dillon are signing papers in my office at nine o'clock in the morning and then you can—"

"Mom? Mom? Aunt Tracy! Something's wrong with Mom!"

The voice came through a tunnel, familiar but far, far away. Every fiber in Amy's body began to shake. Hands grabbed her shoulders. Someone took her phone and said hello. Her vision dimmed and sparked with stars. And then she remembered to draw air into her lungs.

"Amy? Amy! What happened?" The voice was her cousin's. In the background, Tracy squealed into the phone.

Shaking her head cleared a bit more of her field of vision and then her head. The words came back. "Janelle… Janelle is…" Her chest heaved with a sob. "Re-relinquishing her rights to…"

Matt yelled. "Yes! Jana, we're getting adoptized!"

Jana wrapped her arms around Amy's legs. "Don't cry, Mom. Don't cry. It'll be okay."

Amy leaned against the wall to steady herself, then bent and wrapped one arm around Jana and reached out for Matt. "Yes," she gasped, looking up at the picture that hung above the fireplace. Home where it belonged. "It will be okay. Everything is going to be absolutely, wonderfully, miraculously okay."

Dear Reader,

Halfway through writing *The Art of Deception*, I realized how much the subject of fear had crept into the story line. Cozy mysteries aren't necessarily all lighthearted, but I certainly don't want to drag my readers down with too much heaviness. And yet, as I got to know our characters better, I became more confident about letting their struggles with faith over fear unfold.

Most of us will face seasons in our lives when what-ifs loom large. Like Amy, Pearl, and John, we may have days when we have the strength to rest in God's love, knowing He is in control. But interspersed with those times are the days when fear seems almost personified, lurking in the corners, shadowing our every move.

I've lived through several roller-coaster seasons. Fears over finances, a child's illness, or strained relationships can make us feel mired in the mud. During one of those seasons, I saw a poster at a friend's house. It depicted a country road stretching off into the distance. Printed across the horizon was a quote from Corrie ten Boom: "Never be afraid to trust an unknown future to a known God." Those were exactly the words I needed at the time. Twenty-five years later, I'm still repeating them in those top-of-the-roller-coaster-can't-catch-my-breath moments.

Whatever you're facing today, I hope you'll take some time to think about what we know about our God. He is the one who knows the exact number of hairs on your head (Matthew 10:30). He is the one who searches your heart, discerns your thoughts, and knows what you are about to say before you do (Psalm 139). This is also the Heavenly Father who rejoices over you with gladness, quiets you by His love, and exults over you with loud singing (Zephaniah 3:17).

I pray these truths will help you trust your unknown future to a known God.

Blessings,
Becky Melby

About the Author

Becky Melby has written more than twenty books, including four in the Guideposts Secrets of Wayfarers Inn Series. She and her husband, Bill, live in Wisconsin. They have four sons, four daughters-in-love, fifteen grands, and two grandsons-in-love. With eleven granddogs, three grandcats, and more grandducks and grandchickens than they can count, they do not practice the advice Amy is trying out on Matt and Jana: Why own when you can enjoy someone else's and let them clean up the mess? When not writing or spoiling grandkids, Becky can be found chilling behind Bill on their Honda Gold Wing motorcycle or touring the country in their camper. (Unlike our heroines, her tenting days are now in the rearview mirror.)

To connect with Becky, contact her at beckymelby.com, beckymelbybooks@gmail.com, or on Facebook or Instagram.

AN ARMCHAIR TOUR of GRANDMA PEARL'S STOMPIN' GROUNDS

What would it be like to be a fifteen-year-old in Canton, Missouri, in 1937?

Thanks to the influence of Hollywood, 1930s fashion trended toward glamor and sleek silhouettes. As Pearl leafed through women's magazines, she may have dreamed of wearing a Los Angeles-inspired satin evening gown, but the economic reality in Canton in the thirties meant that most women sewed their own clothing and upcycled existing dresses into newer, more stylish frocks. Flour was often sold in pretty fabric bags, and Depression-era women used these to make new dresses and aprons.

Magazine articles with titles like Eight Steps to the Hollywood Face gave tips on how to apply mascara from a cake or bar with a brush. (Liquid mascara did not appear until the 1950s.) Readers were advised to top off their cream eye shadow with a "lovely sheen" of Vaseline, a trick used by Hollywood stars like Marlene Dietrich.

The Top Five songs on the radio in 1937 were:
"It's De-Lovely" – Eddy Duchin
"Goodnight My Love" – Benny Goodman and Ella Fitzgerald
"This Year's Kisses" – Benny Goodman, Helen Forrest
"Marie" – Tommy Dorsey, Jack Leonard, Bunny Berigan
"Boo Hoo" – Guy Lombardo

"Shellac" records (78 rpm) were made of a brittle material containing a shellac resin. Which Top Ten records do you think Pearl would purchase when she could finally afford her "dreamy" RCA Victor Special?

Perusing copies of the *Canton Press-News* from 1937 gives a glimpse into everyday life. Ads touted Black-Draught Laxative for regularity and Dr. Pierce's Favorite Prescription as the cure-all for nerves. While the Cantonbury Tales column exists only in this series, the weekly paper featured a Social News column that reported on bridge club meetings, family reunions, Canton PTA fundraisers, who was in the hospital (and for what), and where local families vacationed.

At the Kroger Store, eggs sold for 24¢ a dozen, coffee was 17¢ a pound, and an angel food cake made with thirteen eggs could be purchased for 35¢. As she was trying to perfect her pie crust skills, Pearl could have gotten a forty-eight-pound bag of Wilson's Best flour for $1.90. While these prices seem great to us, we have to remember that the average yearly wage in 1937 was $1,780.00.

Canton's New Gem Theater had two shows every night at 7:00 and 9:00, and a 2:30 Sunday matinee. Admission was 10–25 cents. Pearl may have watched *Last of Mrs. Cheyney* starring Robert Montgomery, Joan Crawford, and William Powell, which could have been accompanied by a Popeye cartoon and a newsreel, or *Champagne Waltz* with Fred MacMurray, plus an added slapstick feature, *Hoi Polloi* with the Three Stooges.

Pearl and Richard (or Bess) may have ordered two of the 765 varieties of ice cream sodas sold at the grand opening of the Coffee Shop in Canton in July of 1937. Pearl could have taken part in a fall community festival, attended weekly Thursday night concerts in the park, and might have been part of what the local newspaper called "the greatest religious awakening this generation has known" when speakers from the National Preaching Mission visited Canton.

Though Pearl called Canton a "boring town," in reality she would have had much to keep her busy...even before the mysterious stranger with the German accent showed up at her church.

SOMETHING DELICIOUS From GRANDMA PEARL'S RECIPE BOX

Grandma Pearl's Blackberry Dumplings

Blackberry Mixture:
8 cups blackberries
2 cups sugar
1 cup water

Directions:
Mix ingredients together in a large pot and bring to a boil on top of stove over medium heat. Once mixture boils you are ready to start dropping dumplings in. Keep mixture boiling as you drop dumplings in.

Dumplings Ingredients:

2 cups sifted all-purpose flour
1 teaspoon salt
½ tablespoon sugar
⅞ cup solid vegetable shortening (no lard, oil, or butter)

1 egg, beaten
½ tablespoon vinegar
¼ cup cold water

Directions:

Mix flour, salt, and sugar then cut in shortening. Add rest of ingredients, mix well. Roll out dough on floured surface and cut into two-inch strips. Drop each strip in boiling blackberry mixture. Press dough under blackberries with the back of a spoon. Continue until all dough is used.

Do not stir. Let cook for approximately ten minutes after dropping in all strips.

Serve in individual bowls with ice cream and/or whipped cream. Yum!

Read on for a sneak peek of another exciting book in the Secrets from Grandma's Attic series!

Testament to a Patriot
BY SHIRLEY RAYE REDMOND

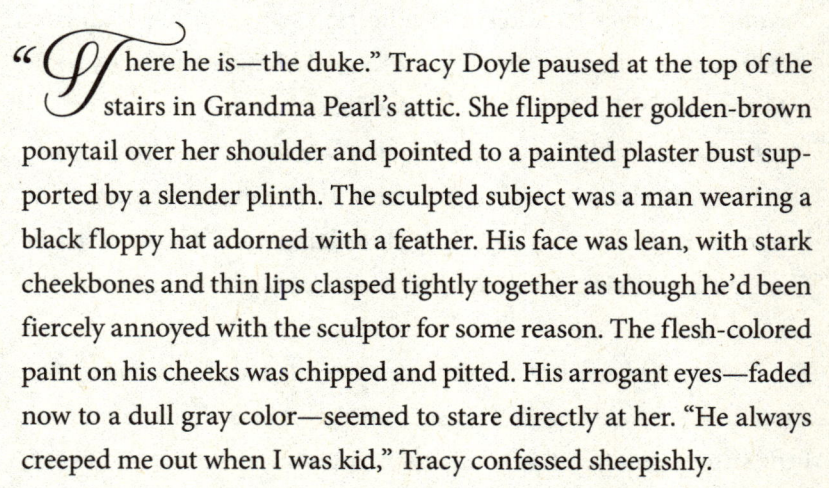

"There he is—the duke." Tracy Doyle paused at the top of the stairs in Grandma Pearl's attic. She flipped her golden-brown ponytail over her shoulder and pointed to a painted plaster bust supported by a slender plinth. The sculpted subject was a man wearing a black floppy hat adorned with a feather. His face was lean, with stark cheekbones and thin lips clasped tightly together as though he'd been fiercely annoyed with the sculptor for some reason. The flesh-colored paint on his cheeks was chipped and pitted. His arrogant eyes—faded now to a dull gray color—seemed to stare directly at her. "He always creeped me out when I was kid," Tracy confessed sheepishly.

With a gurgle of laughter, her younger sister, Amy, admitted, "He still creeps me out. No matter where I stand, he seems to be watching me. I wonder who he was."

Tracy shrugged. "Grandma Pearl didn't know. She said the bust came from Grandpa's side of the family. But I can see why she didn't want this thing downstairs." She gave an exaggerated shudder. "Such a grim face."

After her eyes adjusted to the dimness, Tracy moved past the bust into the sprawling attic, which was filled with an odd assortment of discarded furniture, old crockery, piles of mildewed books, steamer trunks, and crates and boxes of all sizes and shapes. "Are you sure the handkerchiefs are still up here?" she asked, surveying the room.

It was hot and muggy in the attic—but then anywhere in Missouri was hot and muggy in August. Although she wore comfortable cargo shorts and a sleeveless polo shirt, Tracy could still feel the perspiration clinging to her knees and elbows. She hoped Amy would locate Grandma's vintage handkerchief collection sooner rather than later so they could return to the air-conditioned kitchen and enjoy some iced tea and freshly baked snickerdoodles.

Note to self: Bring a window fan up here next time. Tracy stepped past a hulking oak wardrobe with one door hanging off its hinges to make her way to a tipsy floor lamp with a broken shade. She gave the chain a yank. A weak stream of light illuminated the vast space.

"Robin told me it was here," Amy replied with a wheeze. She sometimes suffered from seasonal allergies, and Tracy feared her little sister would pay for the excursion into this dusty realm later on with a sneezy, sleepless night. "The hankies are in a cigar box in one of the old dressers—a cigar box with a Spanish dancer clenching a red rose between her teeth. Or so Robin said."

"What do you need the handkerchiefs for?" Tracy asked.

Amy answered with another sneeze. "They're for a school project. For show-and-tell I want my students to bring something from home that's been in their family for a long time. Or if the thing they want to show is too valuable or fragile, they can show a picture of it. Grandma Pearl's hankie collection is my example for them."

"Sounds like a great way for them to hear some good stories about their parents and grandparents." Tracy used her sneakered foot to push aside an old Gladstone bag covered with a thick pelt of dust. Amy was a creative and dedicated teacher. Tracy thanked the Lord that when Amy was offered a teaching position in their hometown, she had accepted, eagerly returning to Canton with her two soon-to-be-adopted foster children, Jana and Matt, in tow.

This year she'd be teaching first graders at the same elementary school where Sara, Tracy's daughter, taught. School would start soon. Amy had spent considerable time decorating her bulletin boards with colorful posters. Tracy knew she was looking forward to getting back into the classroom.

Amy sighed. "This might take a while. Robin said the box is in one of these bureaus."

There were several hulking bureaus and dressers scattered around the room, including an old cedar chifforobe with half a dozen drawers. Tracy had no idea which piece of furniture to investigate first. Robin would know. Their fun-loving cousin made frequent excursions into Grandma Pearl's attic. Robin loved antiques and had opened her own shop in downtown Canton to indulge her fascination. The attractive store was appropriately named Pearls of Wisdom. It wasn't unusual for potential customers to drive the two and a half hours from St. Louis to Canton just to browse in Robin's shop and enjoy lunch at one of the local diners. If their cousin insisted that Grandma's handkerchiefs were up here in an old dresser somewhere, they surely must be.

While Amy riffled through drawers, Tracy's gaze flitted here and there, settling at last on a stack of books and a shoebox piled on top of a wooden chest nearby. She lifted the shoebox, but then one of the books caught her eye. An old Bible with a dark green cover. She picked it up, set it on the box in her hand, and gently turned the first few pages. The leather binding was limp with age. The pages appeared faintly brown along the edges with a slight tendency to curl at the corners. On the inside cover was a bookplate stating that the Bible had been donated by the Gideons. Tracy knew this wasn't Grandma Pearl's well-loved personal Bible. She'd found that months before and taken it downstairs. In fact, it had been the source of a beguiling mystery when she discovered the name Ezekiel Collins recorded on the "Family Births" page along with the names of Grandma Pearl's own children.

So whose Bible was this? There was no name written inside—just the Gideon bookplate. As Tracy carefully fluttered the pages, they opened easily to the Book of Numbers. Even in the dim light, she couldn't fail to notice several underlined verses and some rather cryptic notations scribbled in the margins. Tracy had a strange feeling—a premonition of something unexpected about to happen. Whether pleasant or not, she couldn't say. She didn't know. But her experience as a reporter for the local newspaper had conditioned her to recognize leads and angles worth pursuing. This was definitely one—she felt it in her bones.

For a moment she stood motionless, the open Bible in her hands, too puzzled to even conjecture the meaning of the underlining and the markings—none of which made any sense at all. They appeared to be nonsensical scribbles. Needing additional light so she could better examine the penciled notations, Tracy walked over to another floor lamp, rusty with age, and turned it on. The bulb was dim, but sufficient. She knew they had Robin to thank for the fact that the lamps worked at all. Their cousin paid attention to little details like replacing light bulbs and setting clove-studded oranges here and there to help cut the musty smell of the cluttered attic.

Tracy held the Bible under the light. What did the mysterious notes mean? Why were these particular verses underlined? Could they have some special significance other than the obvious? She didn't recall her grandmother being particularly fond of this book in the Old Testament. Straightening up, Tracy cast a distracted look around the attic. Amy interrupted her puzzled reverie.

"I found 'em!" Her sister's voice was triumphant as she held out a cigar box for Tracy to see. "Grandma Pearl's hankies." Just as Robin promised, colorful handkerchiefs were folded neatly in an old cigar box with a Spanish senorita on the top. "What's in there?" Amy tipped her chin toward the shoebox still in Tracy's hands. "More hankies, maybe?"

Tracy put the Bible down, lifted the shoebox lid, and saw a stack of faded and ripped-open envelopes, which were far more interesting than vintage hankies any day, in her opinion. "Old letters," she said.

"Maybe they're love letters that Grandpa wrote to Grandma when they were young," Amy said.

Tracy pawed through the contents, selecting a couple of letters at random to slip from their envelopes and scan for a signature. Each letter started with "Dear Pearl" and was simply signed "Love, Peggy." No last name. Underneath the writer's name was a verse from the Book of Numbers. Tracy stood still for a moment, gripped by some formless uneasiness, and then shook it off. A coincidence? Surely not. But who was Peggy? And what did the Bible references beneath Peggy's name mean?

Tracy contemplated the old letters written on thin pink paper, now wrinkled with age. The handwriting was beautifully neat, each cursive letter well formed and precise. All the letters were postmarked 1945. In the upper left-hand corner of each envelope, a Washington, DC street address appeared but not the name of the sender. A first-class postage stamp was only three cents back then. Those were the days!

"Did Grandpa write them?" Amy asked, taking a step closer to peer over her sister's shoulder.

"I don't want to disappoint your romantic little heart, Amy, but these letters aren't from Grandpa to Grandma Pearl." Tracy offered her sister one of the letters and its envelope to read for herself. "Someone named Peggy wrote them from Washington, DC." She opened another letter and scanned the single sheet. "In this one, Peggy writes that she's an office clerk, which is, quote, 'much more interesting than rolling bandages and sewing blackout curtains.' She says that the Washington Monument is grand and the Lincoln Memorial too impressive for words."

Amy refolded the letter she held and placed it back in its envelope. "Hmm, I don't know any Peggys, do you? I don't even recall Grandma mentioning any friends named Peggy. Still, the letters sound intriguing. Let's take them downstairs to read later."

"They're more than intriguing," Tracy said, hastily opening another envelope and examining the letter. It had Peggy's signature, but the line underneath it was blacked out. "In fact, discovering them is a bit weird."

"What's so weird about it?" Amy asked. She wiped a dusty hand on her blue shorts.

"Do you see that Bible?" Tracy pointed. "There are several underlined verses in the Book of Numbers," she explained. "The letters I've looked at all have a reference to the Book of Numbers under her signature, except for one, which is blacked out. See for yourself."

Amy set the hankie box down, retrieved the Bible, and opened it to Numbers. Tracy opened the remaining envelopes. Were there Bible verses underneath Peggy's signature in those letters too? Sure enough, there were. Every single letter had a scripture reference—all from the Book of Numbers in the Old Testament.

To Amy, she said, "Look this one up, okay? Numbers 24:13."

Amy carefully thumbed the pages of the old Bible. "Got it."

"What does it say?"

Amy held the open Bible underneath the dim floor lamp and read, "'If Balak would give me his house full of silver and gold, I cannot go beyond the commandment of the Lord, to do either good or bad of mine own mind; but what the Lord saith, that will I speak?'" She glanced up at Tracy. "What an odd verse for someone to make reference to. What do you think she meant by it?"

"I have no clue." Tracy felt an undeniable misgiving. The verse had to mean *something*. Had Grandma Pearl been equally puzzled by the reference? Had she written the squiggles in the margins of the Bible or had someone else?

"Maybe it's a coded message of some sort," Amy said in a hushed voice, her brown eyes wide. "Maybe this Peggy person was a spy during the war."

"I suppose she could have been," Tracy said without conviction. She searched her memory, thinking how strange it was that she'd never heard Grandma Pearl mention a friend named Peggy. Grandma had been a natural-born storyteller, always willing to share an anecdote from her childhood and "the good old days." Of course, Grandma hadn't mentioned everyone she'd ever met, but this Peggy person must have been someone special. She'd sent Grandma coded letters, hadn't she?

"Maybe Peggy was a code breaker during the war," Tracy mused.

Amy sneezed. "Grandma already knew one code breaker, remember?"

"Elizabeth Blair," Tracy said. "Maybe she met Peggy through Elizabeth or something."

"Can you imagine being a code breaker?" Amy asked. "There was a really interesting documentary about them on one of the history channels not long ago. Matt was very intrigued—you know how he loves a good mystery. I was very happy he got to see how women played such an integral part in the war effort and how their amazing code-breaking skills saved countless lives."

Tracy flicked her sister a doubtful glance. "But that still doesn't explain anything. Grandma Pearl wasn't a code breaker. She was living right here in Canton during the war. Why would this Peggy person write coded letters to Grandma Pearl? And wouldn't she be breaking some sort of military protocol if she did?"

"Maybe it was just for fun." Tracy refolded the letters, returned each one to its proper envelope, and placed them back in the shoebox.

Amy sneezed again then said, "If this Peggy was a spy or a code breaker, do you think Grandma Pearl was spying too? Helping her out in some way?"

Tracy knew that Grandma Pearl had planted a victory garden and had saved her money to purchase war bonds. Grandpa had volunteered for military service immediately following the bombing of Pearl Harbor but was given a medical discharge two years later. He then worked at the ammunition factory in St. Louis. But spying? That was a different ball game all together. Was it even possible?

"No, I don't think Grandma Pearl was a spy. Either she or Grandpa would have told us, don't you think?" Tracy gave her sister a quizzical glance. "He was always bragging about all the things she could do. He was so proud of her."

Amy nodded. "Yes, he was. But Grandpa wasn't here all the time," she pointed out. "He worked round-the-clock shifts at the ammunition plant and came home on weekends. He wouldn't have known everything Grandma Pearl was doing during the week. She might have kept some of her wartime activities a secret from him."

Tracy sighed. "For heaven's sake! Who would she have been spying on in Canton, Missouri? I wish we had Grandma's return letters to Peggy. Besides, we don't even know if this Bible belonged to Grandma. Her name isn't in it. Maybe it belonged to the mysterious Peggy, and Grandma had nothing to do with the notations in the margins."

Amy tucked the box of handkerchiefs under her arm and clicked off the nearest floor lamp. "Wasn't there a prisoner-of-war camp nearby where they kept captured German and Italian soldiers? What if Grandma was spying on someone in the camp—one of the guards, for instance—or one of the prisoners? Or what if the letters were addressed to Grandma and she was supposed to pass them on to someone else? Maybe the mysterious references were really for that other person to decipher."

The two sisters exchanged a glance. Tracy could smell a mystery from a mile off, and this was one she was particularly keen to solve. "I don't know what all this means," she said, scooping up the Bible and the shoebox. "But you can bet your bottom dollar I'm going to find out."

A Note from the Editors

We hope you enjoyed another exciting volume in the Secrets from Grandma's Attic series, published by Guideposts. For over seventy-five years Guideposts, a nonprofit organization, has been driven by a vision of a world filled with hope. We aspire to be the voice of a trusted friend, a friend who makes you feel more hopeful and connected.

By making a purchase from Guideposts, you join our community in touching millions of lives, inspiring them to believe that all things are possible through faith, hope, and prayer. Your continued support allows us to provide uplifting resources to those in need. Whether through our online communities, websites, apps, or publications, we strive to inspire our audiences, bring them together, comfort, uplift, entertain, and guide them.

To learn more, please go to guideposts.org.

Find more inspiring stories in these best-loved Guideposts fiction series!

Mysteries of Lancaster County
Follow the Classen sisters as they unravel clues and uncover hidden secrets in Mysteries of Lancaster County. As you get to know these women and their friends, you'll see how God brings each of them together for a fresh start in life.

Secrets of Wayfarers Inn
Retired schoolteachers find themselves owners of an old warehouse-turned-inn that is filled with hidden passages, buried secrets, and stunning surprises that will set them on a course to puzzling mysteries from the Underground Railroad.

Tearoom Mysteries Series
Mix one stately Victorian home, a charming lakeside town in Maine, and two adventurous cousins with a passion for tea and hospitality. Add a large scoop of intriguing mystery, and sprinkle generously with faith, family, and friends, and you have the recipe for *Tearoom Mysteries*.

Mysteries of Martha's Vineyard
Come to the shores of this quaint and historic island and dig in to a cozy mystery. When a recent widow inherits a lighthouse just off the coast of Massachusetts, she finds exciting adventures, new friends, and renewed hope.

To learn more about these books, visit Guideposts.org/Shop

Sign up for the Guideposts Fiction Newsletter
and stay up to date on the books you love!

You'll get sneak peeks of new releases, recommendations from other Guideposts readers, and special offers just for you...
and it's FREE!

Just go to Guideposts.org/Newsletters today to sign up.

Guideposts. Visit Guideposts.org/Shop or call (800) 932-2145